DID YOU GET WHAT YOU PRAYED FOR?

DID YOU GET WHAT YOU PRAYED FOR?

NANCY JO SULLIVAN
and JANE A. G. KISE

Multnomah®Publishers *Sisters, Oregon*

DID YOU GET WHAT YOU PRAYED FOR?
published by Multnomah Publishers, Inc.

© 2003 by Nancy Jo Sullivan and Jane A. G. Kise

International Standard Book Number: 1-59052-034-3

Cover design by the Office of Bill Chiaravalle
Cover image by Digital Vision

Unless otherwise indicated, Scripture quotations are from:
The Holy Bible, New International Version © 1973, 1984
by International Bible Society, used by permission of
Zondervan Publishing House

Other Scripture quotations:
The Holy Bible, King James Version (KJV)

Revised Standard Version Bible ©1946, 1952 by the Division of Christian
Education of the National Council of the Churches of Christ
in the United States of America
The Holy Bible, New King James Version (NKJV)
© 1984 by Thomas Nelson, Inc.

Multnomah is a trademark of Multnomah Publishers, Inc.,
and is registered in the U.S. Patent and Trademark Office.
The colophon is a trademark of Multnomah Publishers, Inc.

Printed in the United States of America

For information:
MULTNOMAH PUBLISHERS, INC.
POST OFFICE BOX 1720
SISTERS, OREGON 97759

Library of Congress Cataloging-in-Publication Data
Sullivan, Nancy Jo, 1956-
    Did you get what you prayed for? / by Nancy Jo Sullivan and Jane A.G. Kise.
        p. cm.
Includes bibliographical references.
    ISBN 1-59052-034-3
    1. Prayer--Christianity. I. Kise, Jane A. G. II. Title.
    BV210.3 .S85 2003
    248.3'2--dc21   2002151112

03 04 05 06 07 08—10 9 8 7 6 5 4 3 2 1 0

To my grandmother
Mema…you were right.
Sometimes the smallest prayer makes the biggest difference.
Nancy Jo Sullivan

For my daughter, Mari
May you always remember that God is just a prayer away.
Jane Kise

TABLE OF CONTENTS

WHAT IS PRAYER?

The homeless woman stood on the busy downtown corner, the noontime sky darkened with heavy clouds. A damp wind blew through her buttonless coat, while rain soaked the worn canvas of her shoes. Her eyes gazed about aimlessly, dark and empty with despair.

Professionally dressed people rushed toward the surrounding office buildings and restaurants, shielding themselves from the rain with leather briefcases and designer umbrellas. Well-groomed women toting glitzy shopping bags walked a wide perimeter around the lonely woman, not one giving her more than a glance.

Please, Lord...I just need someone to notice me, the woman prayed as raindrops pelted the pavement where she stood. *That's all I'm asking, just someone to notice me.* Secretly she wondered if the petition of a poor, penniless soul like hers could even reach heaven. *Lord, are you still there? I've lost everything. Have I lost You, too?*

At the same time, another woman gripped the steering wheel of her car as she maneuvered through the slippery streets. As she did every day, she prayed, *Please, Lord, let me be the face of Jesus to someone today.* From her car window, she saw the sad-eyed woman standing alone in the downtown throngs, wet and shivering. Without a second thought, she parked her car and ran to the corner. With tenderness she clasped the nameless stranger's hand and looked deeply into her eyes. "How can I help you?" she asked.

The woman's eyes shimmered with tears. "You...you just did," she replied.

Do you wonder if God is hearing your prayers? Do you sometimes feel like that homeless woman, a street-corner stranger on earth, a spiritually poor soul searching for help in your time of need? How can you be sure that an unseen God hears your prayers and surrounds you with His love?

Prayer, conversation with God, *can* provide that assurance. Prayer is the place where you can meet God each day. Prayer is the corner of hope where the words of your heart fly straight to heaven. Prayer is an umbrella of peace. Under its covering, God looks into your eyes and holds your hand and says, "My child, you are precious in My eyes, and I love you."

Over and over, the Bible urges us to pray, yet too often we're stymied by fears that we'll ask for the wrong things or use the wrong words. God doesn't want us to feel alone, homeless, and soaked to the skin as troubles storm around us. He does want us to know that He is always with us, protecting us with His loving presence.

In prayer, God accepts us just as we are. He honors the pleas of His children when we tell Him, "I need You." We do not need perfect petitions in order to move the hand of God. There is no magic formula that will bring answers to our prayers. We can simply follow the lead of the homeless woman: admit we're helpless, be receptive to God's presence, and wait for Him to answer—perhaps in a sudden parting of the clouds, perhaps in the quiet voice of a stranger.

In the pages that follow, you will meet real people who through prayer discovered God on the sacred street corners of their lives. Their varied stories show that every prayer, even the humblest one, holds great power. Prayer is the key that unlocks the door to an abundant spiritual life—not wealth or riches or easy living, but contentment in God no matter what may come.

Our prayer is that this book will enrich your prayer life in a way that lets you *know* that God is listening. That lets you *know* there is always hope in Him. May you discover anew that prayer is the unbreakable cord that connects your heart to heaven.

NANCY AND JANE

CHAPTER 1

WHO HAS TIME TO PRAY?

"The king should issue an edict and enforce the decree that anyone who prays to any god or man during the next thirty days, except to you, O king, shall be thrown into the lions' den."

Now when Daniel learned that the decree had been published, he went home to his upstairs room where the windows opened toward Jerusalem. Three times a day he got down on his knees and prayed, giving thanks to his God, just as he had done before.

DANIEL 6:7, 10

Dear Daniel,

How did you find the courage? If I knew my enemies were waiting to catch me on my knees so they could throw me into a den of hungry lions, I don't know if I could have done what you did. I'd like to believe I'd keep praying, but either I'd make sure I was out of sight, or I'd combine my prayer time with my daily commute so no one could know what I was doing.

At least tell me that you were afraid as you climbed the steps to your upper room, your sanctuary for prayer. Why was it so important? You could have prayed while strolling toward the palace, rolling up your bed mat, or peeling figs. Instead, you went to pray in the one place where they knew they could find you.

And you prayed three times a day. Sometimes I forget to pray at all. I mean to—I even set my alarm clock early to make time for God before the race of the day traps me in its chaos, but somehow my time for Him often gets cut short. Isn't it okay if I pray while tending to chores, driving in the car pool, providing for my family's needs? Isn't God always ready to listen?

Or, Daniel, are you trying to tell me that I don't know what I'm missing? That snatching bits of prayer here and there isn't the same as consciously making room for God? When you climbed those stairs, did you feel as if you were climbing toward God? Maybe you knew that God was waiting to enfold you with love as you expressed your praises and concerns, hopes and sorrows.

I'd like to find an "upper room" in my life, a quiet sanctuary where I could kneel and close my eyes and feel the warm breezes of God. I want to be like you, Daniel. How do I make prayer a priority?

What would our lives be like if we considered prayer as essential as Daniel did? The following stories offer some ideas on how to integrate prayer into our daily lives. The writers discovered that God honors our willingness to set aside time for Him and that "upper rooms" can be found almost anywhere in our lives.

As every day demands its bread, so every day demands its prayer.
No amount of praying, done today, will
suffice for tomorrow's praying.

E. M. BOUNDS

Being with God

JEAN SWENSON

Y ou will never walk again."

I was twenty-eight when I first heard those words. A collision with a semi truck left me paralyzed from the shoulders down. No longer would I be able to engage elementary-age students in exciting learning activities. My hands would never again create works of art, play the piano or guitar, prepare delectable meals, or paddle a canoe. Perhaps most difficult was losing my independence—I now required other people and equipment just to survive.

Lying in bed or sitting in my wheelchair, unable to move, I poured out my heart to God. *Why did this happen? What good is my life now? It's over! I can't do a thing for myself or for anyone else. All I can do is just sit here.*

At times, the grief over my loss seemed overwhelming, but through God's grace and the loving encouragement of family and friends, I continued to believe that God loved me. I clung to the verse, "My grace is sufficient for you, for my power is made perfect in weakness."[1]

Okay, God, I prayed, *I believe that You can still use my life.*

I set about filling my mind with truths from Scripture, especially about God's unconditional love for me. A couple of years after my accident, a friend gave me an audio tape on this very subject. Over and over the speaker emphasized, "You need to know that you know that you *know* God loves you. If you're not sure, ask Him to show you…and He will."

All right, God, I prayed. *If You want to speak to me about this, I'm open. Help me to know that I know that I know You love me.*

Once out of my mouth, that prayer was all but forgotten until a couple of months later. While at a camp for people with disabilities, I met a little girl who was paralyzed and unable to speak. Her soft brown hair was pulled back into a ponytail. She sat rather stiffly—as if she were wearing a brace—in a very small wheelchair that was always maneuvered by the same friendly attendant. Whenever I saw her, I greeted her with a smile.

One afternoon between activities, we had both parked our wheelchairs in a grassy area to enjoy the warmth of the sun. I smiled and nodded at her, and I couldn't help but wonder what she was thinking. How did she view this life that allowed other children to run and play, while she sat motionless in her chair?

On an impulse, I asked her attendant, "May I hold her in my lap?"

"Sure, she's not very heavy."

The attendant gently placed her in my lap, still supporting her, as I didn't have the ability to do so. This precious little girl looked up at me with her big, brown eyes. Suddenly I was overcome with an overwhelming sense of love and compassion toward her. My eyes filled with tears.

I prayed silently. *Lord, this is crazy. Why am I feeling such love for this little girl who can't do a thing for me? All she can do is just sit here.*

Then, clear as day, this thought came into my mind: "Jean, this is exactly how I love *you.*"

I then remembered my prayer to know absolutely that God loves me. My Creator heard me and answered by allowing me to feel for this little girl a portion of His divine love for me. I'm learning that God doesn't care what I can or cannot do—He simply loves me and loves being with me.

⟳

Jean is still traveling life's journey in her wheelchair but has found it to be an incredible platform for sharing God's love and faithfulness.

She also believes that someday, through God's miraculous touch and through spinal cord injury research, she will once again be able to do those things she previously enjoyed. But either way, she still loves spending time with her Lord more than anything.

A Cheerios Revelation

JANE KISE

B eing a mother of one does not necessarily prepare you to be a mother of two.

As a mother of one, I'd had plenty of time to pray. Little Danny slept late almost every morning and took long naps.

But those moments for prayer disappeared when our daughter, Mari, arrived. She simply loved being with people and didn't want to miss a moment of fun, even as an infant. If I arose at 6:30 to snatch a few precious moments of quiet time, Mari awoke at 6:35. I tried getting up at 5:30; at 5:35 I heard her soft coos, which soon became insistent calls. So much for early morning time with God. Afternoons didn't work either since, of course, my children never napped at the same time.

Somewhere during that first year of being a mother to two, my regular time for prayer disappeared. I stayed active in church and joined a once-a-week prayer group, but my daily devotions turned into a reading marathon on Saturdays to catch up with a week's worth of entries. I was sure that God didn't expect more of me, especially since I still volunteered for things like staffing the church nursery for Vacation Bible School.

Running that nursery was no easy task. I was rather proud of my track record of successfully calming every child I'd cared for in church nurseries throughout the years. Infant, toddler, forlorn preschooler—all you have to do is read to them, stack blocks for them to knock down, or bounce them on your knees.

But Vacation Bible School was different. Since most of the VBS teachers were stay-at-home moms, the children in my charge had one thing in common: They were not used to being away from Mommy! On Monday the sobs that filled the air as mothers left were enough to break your heart, but my high school assistant and I had every eye wiped and hand busy by nine-thirty. Tuesday I came prepared with activities, but little spats broke out all morning long.

On Wednesday, despite my best efforts, half of the toddlers were sitting by the door, asking for their mothers, while the other half crowded around my lap, sobbing. I looked at my watch, the clock on the wall, then my watch again. Not yet ten o'clock. I wondered if I'd finally met my match.

As their fussing increased, I brought out my best weapon of defense: snacks. Today's offering was a large bag of Cheerios. The children rushed to sit at the tables as we placed handfuls of Cheerios on napkins in front of each chair. Their little piles disappeared in record time.

"More."

"All gone!"

"Where mine?"

I moved quickly from child to child, replenishing their cereal as fast as I could. In their anxiety over yet another morning at church, had none of them eaten breakfast? I doled out the last of the little o's and sent up a quick prayer. *God, this is turning into a terrible morning. Help!*

Less than a minute later, in walked Corey, the teenage brother of one of the little girls. "I forgot to tell you about the Cheerios in my sister's diaper bag. Since she's already eating, you can share them with the other kids if you want."

With twelve toddlers screeching for more, I found that diaper bag in record time. Inside were as many Cheerios as I had brought for the whole group! I didn't stop to ponder why any mom would pack so much for just one child; I simply started handing them out. Just as I neared the end of that supply, the children gradually slowed in their eating, then wandered away from the tables, ready to play.

A happy hum filled the room where just minutes before

screams had echoed. And in that hum God seemed to say to me, "This morning is like your life: chaos…unless you take time to feed your soul, unless you take time for Me."

But when? How? I prayed for an answer.

Early the next morning when Mari awoke full of smiles and chatter, I pulled her high chair up next to me at the kitchen table. In front of her I placed a handful of Cheerios. In front of me, I opened my prayer journal. She ate, I wrote. Ten minutes for prayer!

The next day I hunted for a new daily devotional that I wouldn't want to skip and placed it by the television. Twenty minutes of *Sesame Street* became twenty minutes of reading and prayer.

I tried taking my journal on trips to the playground. Sure enough, the toy cranes in the sandbox kept my children busy enough for me to pray for a quarter of an hour.

For a few years, I lost the stillness of total solitude in my time with God. Yet with the help of Cheerios and a little creativity, I found that God was *always* waiting for me no matter how I carved out time for prayer.

Now that Jane's children are teenagers and prone to sleeping late, her favorite place and time for prayer is the family room window seat, first thing in the morning. Still, Jane tries to be creative with her prayer life. She keeps a shelf full of different books and journals to maintain variety in her devotional choices. What doesn't change, however, is a mug full of coffee and moments spent simply gazing in thankfulness at God's creation.

One Circle at a Time

Evelyn D. Hamann

I sat on a padded chair toward the front of our church, praying straight from my heart. *O Lord, I love You. I want so much to trust You completely.* I shook my head slowly and tried to inconspicuously wipe a tear that was sneaking out of the corner of my eye. *Even as I speak these words, I still struggle with fear. Please help me to trust You, please!*

As I prayed, I heard the rich harmonies of the visiting musical group up on stage. They were singing a praise song, a melody of joy, but there was no joy in my heart, only pain. I let my hand rest gently on my abdomen. *O Lord, I don't think I can take losing another baby.*

When I first learned of this pregnancy, I was too excited to hold back the news. Out went all the cute little ideas I had dreamed up to reveal my secret to my husband, Scott, and our boys. Instead, I blurted out the news, and we all spent the evening smiling, laughing, and making plans. We were ecstatic.

Scott and I had prayed long and hard about whether to add to our family of four. I yearned to once again feel the soft tender skin of a new little miracle, despite all the work that comes with a baby. But once we'd made the decision, struggles with infertility and two miscarriages followed.

My first doctor visit for this pregnancy had revealed that my hormone levels were low, putting me at high risk for another miscarriage. Several days later, I felt some cramping. The doctor said not to worry; all was probably fine. Since I was in my first trimester, he couldn't do anything other than recheck my hormone levels the following Monday. My anxiety and fear were leading me into feelings of despair and hopelessness.

I tried to pull myself back to the present, to the worship service. One of the women in the group began talking about the children of Israel and their triumph at the wall of Jericho. I had heard this story countless times, but something in her particular description caught my attention.

"God commanded the people of Israel to march around the wall of Jericho once a day for six days. On the seventh day, they were to do it seven times in total silence. Jericho was a large city, and their march would have taken them the better part of a day. They had plenty of time to think as they walked. Perhaps they thought about how much this command didn't make sense. But they knew God, they trusted Him, and they obeyed and walked it one circle at a time...."

One circle at a time! Looking down, I again gently touched my abdomen. *Lord, I think I can do that. I can pray those words every day, like the children of Israel.* Closing my eyes, I made a commitment to spend time in prayer each day, "one circle at a time."

The next morning, I awakened in the calm of prayer. While Scott and the kids slept, I slipped down the hall into the living room and turned on a small light. *One circle at a time, Lord. I can do this. I know You're with me.*

Later that morning, I stopped by the doctor's office for the blood test but had to wait until afternoon for the results. *One circle at a time.*

When the office called with the news that my hormone levels had increased, I could barely find words to reply. As I fumbled to hang up the receiver, new hope grew inside me. *Does this mean I will keep this child, Lord?* One circle at a time. *Okay, Lord, I can do that.*

The next few days I continued to begin my day in prayer, before doing anything else. In the quietness of the living room, I asked God for peace. *I don't understand why You have asked me to walk this road, but if You will help me, I can trust You one circle at a time.* The days turned into a week, and I allowed myself to dream just a little of holding a newborn once again.

Then one evening I headed to a meeting at church. Just as the speaker was about to start, I felt that familiar abdominal tightening. *One circle at a time.* I excused myself to the rest room and saw the first signs of life lost. Instead of bursting into inconsolable tears, I felt calm, with no thought other than to get home.

As I drove, the contractions grew stronger. When I walked in the door, I told Scott what was happening. Concern washed over his face, and he wrapped his arms around me. Then he drew back and looked at me. "Are you all right?"

One circle at a time. "I've been asking myself that all the way home, honey. At first I thought maybe I was in shock or denial. But—I can't explain it because I don't understand it myself—but, yes, I am doing fine." I sensed the comfort of my daily prayer time surrounding me.

It was a long night. With the sunrise, both my baby and my dreams of what might have been were gone. The following days were filled with doctor appointments, tests, and phone calls, but in the midst of it all, I took time to pray. *One circle at a time, one day at a time.* Even my doctor questioned me about my apparent calm throughout the ordeal. I tried to explain to him, but how do you explain something that is just, well, unexplainable?

It's been several years since that miscarriage, but I haven't forgotten its lessons. God knows what tomorrow holds. And daily prayer helps me trust Him "one circle at a time."

⊶━⊷

After trying for a third child for a few more years, Scott and Evelyn decided that God wanted them to concentrate on being great parents to their two little boys. But God had a special surprise in store. Son number three, Kael Hamann, was born August 12, 2002. They're enjoying this unexpected blessing one circle at a time!

KEY:

*An abundant prayer life starts with
making myself available to God.*

Prayer can be as vital for us as it was to Daniel if we find ways to anticipate our times with God the way Daniel did. Habit turns prayer into something essential.

But where do we begin? If your days are already so full that getting up earlier seems genuinely impossible, be creative in finding time for prayer. What pockets of time have you overlooked? For example, when do you wait? Could you bring a devotional to the bus stop or a sports practice? How about putting your Bible near the telephone so you can read it when you're placed on hold?

Try praying as you gaze at your schedule for the day, whether it's on an electronic planner or a crowded kitchen calendar. Could reading your Bible take the place of watching television news or sports? Or at least a portion of that time?

Not all of us have a particular room designated for prayer, but perhaps something else could call you to be present with God. As a reminder to be still, you might place something near your desk or on your dashboard: a picture, a Scripture, a symbol of seeking the heart of God. A friend of ours posts a new verse above her sink each day. Usually, she can pray without interruption as she scrubs away, and she can often memorize the verse before the evening dishes are done.

Take time. Then say, "Lord, I'm here...."

Lord, so many days I hit the ground running, never stopping until my mind and soul are so weary that they've forgotten how to be still, how to wait for You, how to find hope in You. Help my longings for You to become stronger than anything else that clamors for my attention. Remind me to be still, to know that You are my God. Amen.

CHAPTER 2

WILL GOD SPEAK TO ME?

He traveled forty days and forty nights until he reached Horeb, the mountain of God. There he went into a cave and spent the night.

And the word of the LORD came to him: "What are you doing here, Elijah?"

He replied, "I have been very zealous for the LORD God Almighty. The Israelites have rejected your covenant, broken down your altars, and put your prophets to death with the sword. I am the only one left, and now they are trying to kill me too."

The LORD said, "Go out and stand on the mountain in the presence of the LORD, for the LORD is about to pass by."

Then a great and powerful wind tore the mountains apart and shattered the rocks before the LORD, but the LORD was not in the wind. After the wind there was an earthquake, but the LORD was not in the earthquake. After the earthquake came a fire, but the LORD was not in the fire. And after the fire came a gentle whisper.

1 KINGS 19:8–12

Dear Elijah,

I wanted to let you know that I've never thought you were cowardly. I would have fled to a cave hundreds of miles away, too, if Jezebel's army were at my heels! Why, one day you're standing on Mount Carmel, calling down the flames of heaven and proving that your God is the one true God—and just hours later Queen Jezebel's messenger delivers your death warrant. I'm sure you didn't have time to think, let alone pray, as you wrapped a cloak about your face, grabbed your staff, and headed toward the wilderness.

When you trudged across the desert, did you keep looking for a sign, wondering where God was and if you had failed as a prophet? You must have felt so alone as you prayed that God would simply let you die.

When you heard the gentle whisper, though, you knew it was God. I wish God would speak so clearly to me so I couldn't possibly miss the message.

But the whisper wasn't what you expected, was it? Were you looking for God in the wind, then in the earthquake, then in the fire, just like I would have? Yet it was when you listened that God spoke. Is that the key? To be silent, to listen for the gentle whisper of our Creator?

The next time you pray, try listening. Don't be afraid to ask questions or to speak your mind, as Elijah did. But then listen for what God might be trying to say to you. In these stories, you'll meet others who found out that God speaks to listening hearts.

A man prayed, and at first he thought that prayer was talking. But he became more and more quiet until in the end he realized that prayer is listening.

SØREN KIERKEGAARD

Opening My Ears

NANCY JO SULLIVAN

I had just begun my early morning workout at the health club. With my hair pulled back in a ponytail, I was dressed in elastic-waistband sweats and a T-shirt. After a very merry Christmas, I'd put on the ten pounds I'd vowed not to gain.

I programmed the StairMaster machine with an uphill routine. Then Jill walked into the exercise room. Dressed in a sporty tank top and flowered shorts, she was carrying a bottle of Evian water. *I wish I looked like her,* I thought, as I watched Jill start pedaling a stationary bike right next to me.

Jill was an acquaintance. Our nine-year-old daughters were in the same class, and I often saw Jill at PTA meetings and school sports events. However, I had made no attempt to get to know her. A former model, Jill was tall and sleek. Her hair was cut into trendy wisps around her face.

The previous evening, I had seen Jill at a school basketball game. She sat across from me on the gym bleachers while we watched our two daughters passing the ball to one another. I eyed her expensive cashmere coat and snakeskin shoes. My outfit, on the other hand, consisted of faded blue jeans and an oversized sweater—"momwear," as my husband calls it. Even though our budget included money for me to buy myself some new clothes, I still felt guilty about spending money on myself. *The kids need clothes more than I do,* I thought, as I sized up Jill's leather bag and my daughter scored the winning point.

The digital display on my StairMaster began beeping. I had finished the first stage of my step-climb routine. "The girls played a good game last night," Jill said as she shifted her bike into a faster gear. We exchanged small talk about the game, and then Jill started joking about the cost of playing school sports. "I wish garage sales carried basketball jerseys," she said.

"Garage sales?" I asked.

"I buy all my clothes at consignment shops," Jill said before taking a sip from her water bottle.

"You do?" I replied. "But your clothes—they're so nice."

Jill leaned toward me and began whispering as if she were telling me a secret that could not be repeated. "Here's the deal. You can get great clothes if you know where to go."

She told me that her cashmere coat was once owned by a local newscaster. "I bought it for next to nothing." As I huffed my way through my workout, Jill rattled off the names of second-hand shops. "And you can get great jewelry at estate sales," she added.

Over the next few mornings, as the two of us lifted weights, Jill gave me ideas about how to put together a consignment wardrobe. "Find pieces that mix and match. Shop for shoes at outlet stores. Go for a monochromatic look," she advised.

Soon my "momwear" found its way to the back of my closet as I replaced it with trendy pants, skirts, and blouses. Though I wasn't spending much money, I was starting to feel more confident about myself.

"You've helped me so much," I told Jill one morning as I walked into the exercise room, my hair cut into a short bob that flipped up on the sides.

Jill and I were becoming friends—good friends. I looked forward to our daily workouts.

Then one morning, Jill paused for a moment before adjusting her treadmill. Her eyes were filled with sadness. "Today is the anniversary of my little brother's death," she said. The two of us began power walking on side-by-side treadmills while she explained that years earlier her seven-year-old brother had been killed in a tragic accident. "After he died, my faith in God died, too," she said, her voice somber.

I didn't know what to say. *Tell her about your faith,* an inner voice suggested. Though I was sure that God had spoken, I quickly dismissed the prompting. *This is a health club,* I reminded God. *It's not the right time or place to share such personal things!* Still the inner voice persisted. *Tell her about Me.* I refused to listen. *Faith is a private thing,* I reasoned to myself.

The next morning, after we had finished exercising, Jill invited me over to her house for coffee. "I want to show you something," she said. When I stepped into her entryway, Jill pointed to a sculptured stone image that hung on her wall, right next to the doorway. I studied the old work of art; it was an image of Jesus knocking on the door of a vine-covered cottage. "I picked it up yesterday at an antique shop. What does it mean?" she asked.

A passage I had memorized as a child came to mind, and I recited it. "Behold, I stand at the door and knock. If anyone hears My voice and opens the door, I will come in to him and dine with him, and he with Me."[2]

Jill looked at me curiously. Once more I felt a divine nudge. *Tell her about Me.* This time I listened and said, "God's knocking on the door of your heart."

It's been almost a year since Jill bought that sculptured picture. She and I continue to meet every morning at the health club. We still talk about our kids and fashion, but these days we find ourselves focusing on God, exchanging requests for prayer, and encouraging one another in faith. In many ways we've become spiritual lifelines for one another.

I'm grateful for Jill's presence in my life. Together we've learned that our friendship is a gift from God, one that has transformed both our lives. We've also learned that great things happen when we take the time to hear God knocking at the door of our hearts. All we have to do is listen.

A few weeks after Nancy wrote this story, Jill called. The antique sculpture had been accidentally broken beyond repair. Knowing how much the wall sculpture meant to Jill, Nancy immediately began praying for a replacement. Just a few days later, while shopping at a neighborhood garage sale, Nancy spied an exact replica of the sacred sculpture—and it was only fifty cents!

Sixty-Two Dollars

BY NANCY H. CRIPE

I was unpacking after a move when I found the check lying in the bottom of my wooden trunk. Dated almost twenty years ago, the writing on the check had faded, but I could still read my signature and the amount: sixty-two dollars. Holding that canceled check in my hands was like stubbing my toe on a biblical stone of remembrance. I sat down on the floor, forgetting my unpacking, and relived a long-ago prayer and the Lord's double answer.

During my senior year of college, I lived in a house with a group of Christian women. A wise, older Christian friend gently challenged me about the practice of tithing. She encouraged me to try out God's faithfulness by giving. Living on a student's tight budget, I saw no way to give.

One Friday night at the end of the fall semester, I sat down to straighten out my accounts before going home for Christmas. I paid my rent, my tuition, and my car payment. Amazing—there was still money left! So I hesitantly figured 10 percent of my autumn earnings for my first-ever tithe. If I *did* tithe. If I *dared* tithe. The calculator numerals glowed red with the amount: sixty-two dollars.

I thought of all the other ways I could use the money, especially over the holidays. *Lord, I want to give this money to You. But does such a small amount really matter, even though it's a lot to me? What difference can it make? What if I end up needing it?*

Trust me, God's Spirit seemed to prod. *Someone else needs this money more than you do.* So with a mixture of reluctance, obedience, and expectation, I wrote one more check, for sixty-two dollars. I planned to put it in the collection plate at church on Sunday, because that's as much as I knew about tithing: You put the money into God's hands and let Him do the rest.

Later that night when I went upstairs to my room, I heard sobs coming from behind a friend's closed door. I gently knocked. "Lisa, can I come in?"

"Just a minute." I heard her blow her nose, and then she opened the door, wiping her puffy eyes with a tissue.

"I was going to bed, and I heard you crying and, well, you sounded so sad. Do you want to talk?" On her desk I saw an end-of-semester pile of bills and checkbook statements similar to what I had just waded through.

She slumped into her chair and held her head in her hands.

"I've never done this before," she cried. "I'm usually so careful about my finances, but with finals I didn't keep track very well and—" Lisa's voice broke. "I'm so ashamed," she whispered. "My bank account is overdrawn."

I sat down on her bed, inwardly relieved that it was only money. She wasn't crying about a breakup with her fiancé, dismal semester grades, or difficulties in her spiritual journey. This problem was so fixable. "How much?" I asked.

"Sixty-two dollars! A week's earnings at my campus job…"

I was stunned. No words would come. Then my shock turned into a beaming smile. "Really? Sixty-two dollars? That's amazing!"

Puzzled over my cheerfulness, Lisa's face filled with hurt. I hurried to explain. "I'm not smiling about your bookkeeping, Lisa. I'm smiling about God's incredible overdraft protection, right down to the dollar. Hold on; I'll be right back."

When I returned with my checkbook and explained about the check I'd written earlier, Lisa looked at me in disbelief. "I can't take it. This money is for the church or missions or somebody who needs it."

"You need it, Lisa. Besides, it's not my money or yours; it's God's."

I opened my checkbook, voided the first sixty-two-dollar check, and wrote a second one. "When your finances get squared away, you can give the sixty-two dollars back to God. For the church or missions or somebody who needs it." I handed her the check. "I think this is the Lord's idea of a loan!"

My prayer earlier that night had been for the courage to trust God to provide for me. I hadn't imagined that I'd be given the privilege of seeing my faltering steps of obedience provide relief and rescue in the name of Christ. I tucked away that voided check in my trunk as a stone of remembrance—sixty-two dollars, a December prayer, and two young women drawn closer to a God who provides.

<hr />

After years of teaching high school biology, Nancy's life now centers around her husband and two young children. Old devotional books, long walks, and great friends all encourage her to keep trusting God. Nancy's experiment with tithing continues two decades and three calculators later. One of the best lessons of tithing for her has been learning to listen to God—where to give, to whom, and for what. In big and small ways, Nancy has learned that it's impossible to outgive the Giver of all good gifts.

The Gift of a Day

VICKI MANUEL

The day before Mother's Day that year was one of those splendid spring days that insists you shed shoes and jacket and simply glory in blossoms and sunshine. But I scarcely noticed the brilliant blue skies or my neighbor's pink apple blossoms. Head down, I gathered a bouquet of lily of the valley from under the oaks in our backyard, wrapping the stems in wet paper towels and a plastic bag for the trip to the nursing home. All the while I wondered if Mom would even be able to appreciate their ethereal fragrance.

I didn't want to admit, even to myself, how tired I was of visiting her. A series of small strokes had taken what twenty-five years of arthritis couldn't wrest from her spirit. Now she seldom even wanted to move from her bed to her wheelchair. She couldn't form words; our visits consisted of my small talk and her hand gestures. Often she didn't recognize me, and the joy had disappeared from her smile. *Lord,* I prayed, *this hurts so much. Why are You keeping her alive?*

Mom was now such a pitiful contrast to the mother I had known. She'd been so determined to make the best of things. She never complained through the rounds of surgeries and medicines her arthritis demanded. Even when her hip replacement surgery was unsuccessful, she joked about the painful leather brace she had to wear. One time we were playing cards, and she kept fidgeting with the brace, trying to get comfortable. I said, "You must be ready to burn that thing."

"Why, honey, no," she said, leaning forward a bit. "I'm so thankful the doctors had something that could help me. Otherwise where would I be?"

That was Mom, insisting that life was good, to be enjoyed.

35

Even when her rheumatoid arthritis worsened, robbing her of playing the piano, baking bread, and cracking open pistachios for my daughters, she insisted, "I'm still thankful, for just anything and everything! I still have you, my granddaughters, and that wonderful son-in-law!"

But now that spirit was gone. Now when I visited Mom, she was usually either sleeping or lying down. I wondered if she even knew I was in the room. As I drove over that day before Mother's Day, I kept asking God why she was still alive. Only a shell remained of the vibrant woman she'd been.

When I opened the door to her room, the sunlight streaming through the windows took me by surprise. Before I even spotted Mom, she said, "Oh hi, honey." Another surprise. She was sitting up in her wheelchair instead of lying in bed.

"Uh…hi. Happy Mother's Day," I said. I stared at her. Had I imagined her greeting? She was not only up, but also dressed in a knit skirt and bright velour top. I kissed her cheek and handed her the lilies of the valley. She grasped them clumsily in her twisted hands and then breathed in their fragrance. "They've always been my favorite," she said.

I was startled by that complete sentence, her first in months. What was going on? I put the flowers in a vase I'd brought along, then knelt down beside Mom's wheelchair and reached for her misshapen hands. I wondered what to say next. For months I'd made up one-sided conversations, not expecting or receiving answers. I finally said, "It is just beautiful outside. Would you like me to take you for a walk?"

She answered, "Oh, I wish your dad could bring my coat. I don't have a coat." I checked her closet, found a sweater, and assured her that she'd be fine with the sweater and a blanket. Cautiously, I wheeled her out into the hall, not sure if this was a good idea. How long could she sit up? When was she last out of bed? I had no idea.

I steered Mom's chair through the maze of doors and hall-ways. We soon passed through the glass doors of the entryway, out of the hospital smells, and into the glorious spring day. Mom immediately spotted the flowering crab trees, their delicate pink blossoms at the peak of their bloom. She exclaimed, "Aren't those trees beautiful!" and she leaned forward, taking in her first glimpse of the world in months.

Mom's coherent sentences stripped away the gloom that had trapped my spirit. I pushed her chair up the dandelion-covered hill and along the boulevard. Mom pointed. "Look! Here are the dandelions. They remind me of when you were little."

So I picked a bouquet for her, as I had so many times as a girl. She clasped them tightly in her knobby hands, and we con-tinued down the sidewalk. Her head turned right, then left, then back again, as if she didn't want to miss a single sight.

A stream of water raced along the curb. "Where is all the water coming from?" Mom asked.

"It rained last night, Mom. Quite a bit."

"Wait; aren't those violets? Look at those violets." I stopped, locked the brake on her chair, and picked a bouquet of the tiny Johnny-jump-ups she'd spotted.

We continued along, my mom delighting in things I might have rushed right by—the hodgepodge of mailboxes on the cor-ner, a bright red car, a boy out shooting baskets. A bee came by, and she tried shooing it away with her bouquet. "That bee smells your dandelions, Mom."

"And my Johnny-jump-ups!" With that, her hands relaxed their grip on her flowers. I knew she was getting tired, so I headed back to the nursing home.

I got her back to her room, helped her into bed, and watched her promptly close her eyes. I left the room to get some water. When I returned, she opened her eyes and said, "We had a wonder-ful time, didn't we, honey?"

"Yes, we did, Mom. I love you."

"I love you, too," she replied and again closed her eyes. I stayed until she was fast asleep, my hand covering her gnarled fingers. Contentment washed over me with the same sweetness as the flowers perfuming the room.

That was it. Mom lingered another five months, but she never spoke to me again. It didn't matter. On that day when I had questioned why God was keeping her alive, He gave me a gift, an answer I continue to cherish. My mother's delight in every flower and every blade of grass she saw that day convinced me that life is always worth being thankful for. And I am.

⊷━⊶

Vicki shared this story at the celebration of her mother's life, a life that was a gift to the many people she touched. Another aspect of God's answer to Vicki is knowing that the flowers of spring will always bring back wonderful memories of her mother.

KEY:

God speaks if we're willing to listen.

When you're conversing with a great friend, time just flies. That's the way the Creator of the universe wants to converse with you, as a loved one you can meet with anyplace, anytime. Prayer is conversation, not a monologue.

But listening takes time, especially to create the kind of stillness where you can hear even if God comes in a whisper. Here's an idea. Sit down as you would for a long chat with a good friend. Picture Jesus sitting with you. Tell Him your hopes, your fears, your dreams. Ask questions. That's all part of a good conversation. And then be still. Relax in God's presence, and listen with your heart. Even if you don't hear anything, savor the silent communion with Him.

Be open to the different ways your prayers might be answered. You might want to write down each of your concerns, then list what possibilities come to mind. Someone to call? A book to read? A Scripture verse? The answers may come in the events of the day, in your conversations with others, or through new insights into your problems. Perhaps there won't be a thunderous answer, but rather a still, small voice. Just be sure to listen. And in the listening, you will develop a rich closeness with God, a newfound intimacy that will satisfy your heart's deepest desires.

Lord, before a word is on my tongue, You know it completely.[3] Yet so often I try to do all the talking. Help me to listen to You, to be attentive to Your voice, and to be courageous enough to wait for Your answers. Amen.

CHAPTER 3

ARE MY PRAYERS SELFISH?

"What do you want me to do for you?" Jesus asked him.

The blind man said, "Rabbi, I want to see."

"Go," said Jesus, "your faith has healed you." Immediately he received his sight and followed Jesus along the road.

MARK 10:51–52

Dear Bartimaeus,

After reading the story about how Jesus restored your sight, I went outside and closed my eyes, trying to imagine myself as a beggar, two thousand years ago on the streets of Jericho. You didn't know what a daffodil looked like, or the thrill of watching the effortless soar of an eagle against an azure sky.

Even worse, people ignored you, didn't they? You must have felt like half a person. No wonder you cried out, "Jesus, Son of David, have mercy on me!" The crowd told you to be quiet, but Jesus stopped and asked you what you wanted from him. "Teacher," you said, "I want to see!"

When I opened my eyes again, I pretended it was the first time I had seen the soft blues of the sky, the dozens of greens that make up grass. And to think that your first sight was of Jesus. No wonder you followed Him down the road toward Jerusalem!

Someone once told me that asking God for things for myself is the lowest form of prayer. Instead, I should concentrate on praying for other people and their needs. But your story is different. It tells me that I can ask for God's gifts.

And I'm struck by the fact, Bartimaeus, that God didn't restore your sight for just your benefit. How many people saw God's love in a new way after hearing your story? Surely you told anyone who would listen! And I can just imagine the joy that sparkled from those eyes of yours that Jesus gifted with His touch. ...

Jesus suggested that we approach God with a childlike faith. Pray as if you were making a request of a loving parent who not only gives you what you need but also hopes to bring you joy. Yes, God helps us see any selfishness behind our requests. But as the following stories show, we often learn through prayer about the abundance of God's loving care for us. For some, it's like seeing the face of their loving Father for the first time.

At all times let us believe that man's prayer on earth and God's answer in heaven are meant for each other.

ANDREW MURRAY

The Piano

SHARON SHEPPARD

I learned how to spell the word *yearn* in fourth grade. But I'd been doing it long before I knew how to spell it. Some girls dream about having a bicycle or a horse. I dreamed about having a piano and knowing how to play it.

The closest I could come to having one was sitting near the front of the church every Sunday and watching Caroline Bundy's fingers fly over the keyboard. She dressed up "The Old Rugged Cross" so much that I hardly recognized it. I watched her. I listened to every note. Then one day I said to myself, *I could do that.*

On a piece of brown wrapping paper, I drew myself a life-size keyboard. I crayoned in the black keys in sets of two and three. When I finished my makeshift piano, I played. I could hear the songs in my head as my fingers rippled up and down that paper keyboard.

Sometimes on Sunday afternoons, I made my own instrument out of water glasses. I took eight tumblers out of the cupboard—still warm from the dishpan—and filled them with graduated amounts of water. I turned them into a scale and then used a spoon to tap out all of the hymns we had sung in church that day.

When I wasn't playing my make-believe piano, I was playing with my best friend, Shirley. Shirley had a piano at her house, and every chance I got, I tried it out. Making beautiful music wasn't as easy as Caroline made it look. But I plunked around until I could play a tune or two.

After church one Sunday, I scooted up to Mama and whispered my secret in her ear. "I can play the piano!" I said. "Will you stay after everybody leaves and let me show you?"

"Sure, honey," she said, then went right on talking to Mrs. Harris.

Finally, when everyone had left, I led Mama up to the front pew, and I slid onto the piano bench. I didn't know the names of any of the notes, but in my head I knew what the keys sounded like. I stumbled through "The Way of the Cross Leads Home," which I played on the black keys.

My mother looked a little surprised. "That's wonderful, honey! How did you ever learn to do that?"

I just shrugged.

That afternoon I overheard Mama say to Daddy, "We really need to see what we can do about getting Sharon a piano."

My heart pounded.

"That would be mighty nice, Esther, but you know we can't afford it right now."

I sighed, because I knew that was the truth. But for a minute there, I was hoping he'd say, "You're right. Let's start looking for a good used piano."

That Sunday the pastor preached about envy. I felt guilty all afternoon because I wanted to play like Caroline. I was envious, pure and simple. *If only I had a piano,* I told myself, all the while trying to pray. *Help me not want a piano. I don't want to be selfish, God.*

But eventually my desire for a piano overcame my worries about being selfish. I prayed earnestly. *Dear God, I know there are starving children in Africa who can't even afford a sweet potato, so it seems pretty greedy of me to ask, but I'm going to do it anyhow. You know I've never wanted anything so much, and I'll try not to make a habit of asking, but if it isn't too sinfully selfish, could I please have a piano?*

Two weeks later, Shirley came over with the best and worst news I'd ever heard.

"We're moving to Northhome," she said. At first I thought she was kidding.

"Northhome?" I said. "There's nothing but ice and snow up there." (As if there was anything but ice and snow where we lived.)

"The railroad is transferring my dad."

"But you can't just leave!"

"I don't have a choice," she said. Suddenly a couple of tears trickled down her cheeks, and I knew she wasn't joking. Reality squeezed my heart. I was about to lose my best friend. I felt lonely already.

I didn't want to talk about it anymore. I couldn't look her in the eye. For the first time in my life, I wished she would go home. I wanted to be alone so I could cry.

"Dad says you can have our piano," she said quietly as she headed for the door. I looked at her curiously.

"What did you say?"

"My dad says you can have our piano when we move."

I think my heart stopped for a minute or so. I had to catch my breath.

"Really?"

"Really," she said. With that, she edged out our back door. I watched as she cut across the neighbor's yard, walking slowly and wiping her eyes with her mittens.

I slipped into my room and soaked my pillow with a gallon of tears. It was a little like eating sweet pickles. You're not sure whether you like them or hate them. They're a little too sour and a little too sweet to be good. While my cheeks were puckering just thinking about it, I couldn't tell which tears were sad ones and which were happy.

The day before Shirley and her family moved, it was fifteen below zero. It took four men to lift and carry the piano into our living room. I was trying it out before Mama could mop up the melting snow the movers had left behind.

It didn't matter that the piano was old and out of tune. It didn't matter that some of the keys stuck. It was a gift of love from a treasured friend.

Today, playing the piano still brings me great joy as my fingers dance across "real" keys. With one piano, God gave me a reminder of dear Shirley, a way to fill my home with music the rest of my life, and an avenue for my heart and soul to reach to the heavens. God knew my yearning wasn't a selfish request—it was a path to faith.

God has continued to bless Sharon through music. Now a retired English teacher, she has found new joys and challenges as a beginning violin student!

Those Cherry Macaroons

SHARON KNUDSON

S tirring the dough for a batch of cookies, I savor the aroma of almond flavoring. I pause to nibble on a few flakes of coconut before adding the maraschino cherries and a handful of crunchy nuts.

Vivid memories propel me back five years.

I was attending a retreat in Colorado after having saved all year for it. Exhausted and desperately in need of rest, I had concluded that this would be a safe place for a single middle-aged woman to recuperate.

The spectacular scenery, delicious food, and rich fellowship helped ease my fatigue. Best of all were the words of the main speaker. His message found a home in my heart and reminded me that God loved me. All week I soaked my weariness in his teaching.

After the final session, I approached the speaker to thank him. We chatted for a while, and he must have noticed the heaviness that hovered around me, because he said to me, "Tell me your story...."

I gave him the condensed version. My thirty-year marriage had ended several years earlier, and I was still grieving the loss. My daughters were both grown and gone—one overseas and the other out on the West Coast. I was working four jobs to make ends meet; the combined incomes gave me just enough to keep my modest home.

Two years of this, however, had left me gaunt and pale. My prayers to God were constant as I fought to keep my fear in check. I also had a bad case of self-pity that I didn't know how to shake.

When I finished talking, the speaker calmly prayed for me—but then he abruptly changed his tone.

"Imagine there's a big book lying open on your lap," he said, suddenly animated. "You've just finished a long, complicated chapter in your life, but now it's over! It's time to finish that section and turn the page."

I balked for a moment...then realized he was right. Slowly, bravely, I turned the page in that imaginary book.

"Now, what do you see? And who is in that chapter?"

Who? There was no "who"! All I envisioned in my future was work, work, work.

"Could there be a man who wants to come into your life?" he asked.

I was shocked. In my mind, there was no man. I wanted nothing to do with that!

The speaker waited in silence.

"Well," I finally said, "there is this one man in the church where I'm the organist, but I certainly have no romantic feelings toward him...." I could feel my face turning a fiery shade of red! I was referring to Bob, a quiet bachelor in his fifties. Known for his kindness and integrity, he had been president of the congregation for many years. While I found it easy to discuss church business with him, there was never any hint of personal interest—only occasional sidewise glances from across the congregation on Sunday mornings....

"Does Bob have a good reputation?" the speaker asked. "Do you wonder why he never married?"

I was embarrassed by his line of questioning, but he was relentless. Finally he asked, "Well, what do you think?"

"I don't know...," I proffered, "but...I do know...I could bless his life."

I couldn't believe what I'd just said! Suddenly I was almost giddy.

The speaker sat back in his chair, folded his arms across his chest, and grinned.

"There you have it," he said. "Maybe God has something in store for the two of you."

I quickly reminded him that I wasn't looking for a man— that I had no intention of pursuing anyone. How selfish it would be to pray for a husband!

"Well, this is what I think you should do," he said. "Go home and bake a batch of cookies. Put some on a nice plate—not a paper plate, but one that must be returned. Give them to Bob next Sunday and say, 'I baked some cookies and thought you might like some.' That's it—say nothing else."

I had no words whatsoever. It sounded too drastic for me!

"You said Bob was a bachelor. Well, there's nothing more appealing to a bachelor than something homemade. Yet there's no manipulation in this plan. Bob can eat those cookies and merely return the plate—or, if he likes, he can take a step toward you. Either way, you've opened the door just a crack. Things could proceed or stop dead in their tracks—it'll be up to Bob."

The retreat came to a close, and I went back home. All day Saturday I wondered if I should bake those cookies. The words repeated themselves over and over in my mind: "I baked some cookies and thought you might like some.…"

How foolish, I thought—yet it might be the perfect thing!

Finally, late that night, I paged through my recipes. There it was: cherry macaroons. Not your ordinary, everyday cookie, but still hearty enough so a man would like them.

I measured the ingredients, stirred in the cherries, and baked them. Then I arranged a few on a translucent pink plate and cov-ered them with plastic wrap, ready to take to church the next day.

Throughout the long service, I was in agony. Surges of panic, wave after wave. *Oh, Lord,* I prayed, *have I done the right thing, or am I acting out of my own selfish desires? Again, I place my future in Your hands. I only want Your will for my life.*

Finally, after coffee hour, the masses started to leave. Shaking,

I approached Bob, thrust the cookies at him, and blurted, "I baked some cookies and thought you might like some!"

Beet red, I turned and fled down the hall. I ran down the steps and out the front door. All the way home I cried. *How could I have humiliated myself like that? What on earth must that poor man be thinking?*

Days passed.

No word from Bob.

And then, on Friday night, he called. He said he'd been weeding the marigolds in his yard.

My goodness, I thought, *a man who likes flowers. And he has a yard.*

Bob made more brief conversation, and then…

"Thanks for the cookies. They were delicious. I'll return the plate to you on Sunday.… Uh…would you, perhaps, care to join me for lunch afterward—if…if you aren't busy?"

There it was—Bob's hand on the door that I had so slightly cracked open. He was opening it further, and I found myself relieved. In fact, it was fine!

The years since have brought many changes. I've thanked God repeatedly for the gift of a whole new life—like a brand-new chapter in a great big book.

The kitchen timer rings and I take the hot cookie sheet out of the oven.

"Come and have a snack, Hubby," I call to Bob. "I made your favorite cookies—cherry macaroons."

⚬—✦—⚬

Bob and Sharon are enjoying a Christ-centered marriage and still marvel at the amazing way God answered their prayers. They are active in two Bible study groups at their church and have coached other groups as well. Sharon is an active speaker and coleads a training program for mentoring women in spiritual matters. She continues to be amazed at how God has transformed her, giving her a whole new life after she "turned the page."

PS: The speaker who counseled Sharon was Bruce Wilkinson, who went on to write *The Prayer of Jabez, Secrets of the Vine*, and *A Life God Rewards*.

Cherry Macaroons

Cream together:

½ cup (1 stick) unsalted butter

½ cup shortening

Gradually add 1 cup granulated sugar, creaming well.

Add:

2 large eggs

1 teaspoon pure almond extract

Beat well.

Blend in:

2 ½ cups all purpose flour

1 teaspoon baking powder

1 teaspoon salt

Add:

½ cup maraschino cherries, drained and diced

2 cups shredded or flaked coconut

1 cup pecans or walnuts, chopped

Mix well and drop by rounded teaspoonfuls onto lightly greased baking sheets. Top each cookie with a quarter maraschino cherry. Bake 12–15 minutes at 350 degrees until lightly browned. Makes 5–6 dozen.

Dreams of Israel

NANCY JO SULLIVAN

Israel. The shiny black letters were set against the bright yellow background of the brochure. It was posted prominently on the bulletin board in my college cafeteria. With a backpack flung over my shoulder, I scanned the posted ad while drinking coffee from a Styrofoam cup. "Come travel with us. Come see the Holy Land," the flyer read. Memories from my childhood flooded back.

I remembered sitting with my family at church when I was ten years old as the pastor showed slides of Israel. Enchanted, I memorized each sacred place: the rough terrain of the Jordan River, the aqua blue of the Mediterranean Sea, the white stones that framed the tomb of Jesus.

"Please, Lord, let me see Israel someday," I had prayed.

The memory quickly faded as I glanced at my watch. Jotting down the phone number on the brochure, I rushed off to a lecture.

Later in my dorm room, I couldn't concentrate on my studies. Instead, I held the phone number in my hand. I wanted to call, but an international trip was not in my budget. I was working my way through school, subsidizing financial aid with the meager wage of a waitress.

I picked up the phone anyway. *It won't hurt to call,* I told myself.

A youth pastor answered. He was happy to share the Israel itinerary.

"How much does the trip cost?" I asked.

"A thousand dollars," the pastor replied.

"I'm sorry," I said. "I can't afford it."

"I won't be needing payment until July 1. That will give you three months," he said kindly. I could tell the pastor sensed my disappointment. "Maybe God wants to work a miracle for you.

Why don't you pray about it?"

"That would be asking God for a miracle," I muttered as I hung up the phone. I'd never thought of asking God for something as big as a miracle. My daily prayers had always been generic: "Lord, bless my family, protect my friends, help me with this exam.…"

How could I ask God for a thousand dollars? God needed to tend to those whose needs were greater than mine—the poor, the lonely, the starving of the world.

I crumpled the phone number and threw it into the waste-basket. For hours I tried to distract myself with homework, but I kept hearing the pastor's words: "Why don't you pray about it?"

Soon I was on my knees, head bowed, hands folded. "Lord, I'm sorry for asking for so much. I know You are busy answering more urgent prayers, but I'd like to go to Israel."

The weeks passed, and I prayed every night that God would provide a way to finance the trip. Though my intercessions were heartfelt, I always apologized for my request. *I know this is a lot to ask, Lord,* I would pray.

The first day of July arrived. I woke up early just as the sun was rising but lingered in bed for a while. I was staying at a girl-friend's house in a guest room decorated with white linens and a silver wall cross.

It's the last day to turn in money, I reminded myself. A Bible lay on the nightstand. I opened it and began reading a passage from the book of Ezekiel. "Go now to the house of Israel and speak my words to them. You are not being sent to a people of obscure speech and difficult language, but to the house of Israel."[4]

Could the words be meant for me? I closed my eyes. *Lord, give me faith to believe that You can still work a miracle.*

Minutes later, my friend knocked on the door. "Let's go out to breakfast," she suggested.

On the way to the restaurant, my friend pulled into the driveway of a steepled church. "I'll be right back; I've got to drop something off," she told me.

As I waited in the car, I looked toward the garage of the church rectory. Inside, I saw a tall man in a flannel shirt fixing a bicycle. I recognized him. He had often ridden past the college, and we had waved to each other many times.

I walked toward the garage and exchanged small talk with the man. I found out his name was Lenny and that he was a seminarian. He wanted to be a pastor and was living at the church for a year.

His commitment to God had compelled him to live a life of simplicity. He had pared down his possessions, giving his car to a homeless man. He dreamed of serving the poor in a third world country.

"God gives generously so we in turn can do the same," he told me as he oiled the chain of his bike.

I grew quiet.

His simple lifestyle seemed to contradict my fervent prayers for a thousand dollars. Was I wrong in asking God for so much?

"So what are your plans for the rest of the summer?" Lenny asked.

"I think…I'm…going to Israel," I said. I told him how I had always hoped to see the Holy Land. "There's a trip scheduled for August. I can't afford it, but I've been praying for a miracle," I said.

Lenny gave the tire on his bike a test twirl. "How much do you need?" he asked.

"A thousand dollars."

Lenny smiled. "You've been praying that God would answer a prayer of yours, and I've been praying that God would answer a prayer of mine."

He explained that he had recently inherited a large sum of money and that he'd been asking God to show him what to do with it.

"But last week," he said, grinning, "I received an additional inheritance of a thousand dollars. Ever since, I've been asking God who it's for."

At first I didn't understand what he was saying.

"That person is you," Lenny said.

"Me?"

He nodded. "You!"

Minutes later, Lenny handed me a one-thousand-dollar check dated July 1.

"How should I repay you?" I asked.

Lenny wasn't at all concerned. "Pay it back to someone who needs it more than I do," he said.

So that August I went to Israel. I hiked along the rocks of the Jordan River, I swam in the cool aqua blue waters of the Mediterranean Sea, and I smelled the fragrant roses that framed the garden tomb of Jesus.

As I trod the homeland of God, I couldn't stop thinking about Lenny's generosity. By sharing an unconditional gift, Lenny had displayed the love of a gracious God who gives without measure or limits. It was a brand of giving I hoped to model for a lifetime.

Twenty years later, I haven't forgotten my commitment. When I'm presented with unexpected opportunities to help people in need, I remember the words of Lenny, now a missionary to the poor of the third world: "God gives generously so we in turn can do the same."

When Nancy first wrote this story, she used a pseudonym, concerned that people might think she was selfish in asking to go to Israel. But she's stopped apologizing to God for grand requests. After all, the answers are always up to Him!

KEY:

God is the provider of good gifts!

Occasionally, others may tell you that making personal requests of God—petitionary prayer—is the lowest form of prayer. They would have us do nothing but praise God and pray for others.

But prayer also helps God mold our hearts. Sometimes we don't know what we need until we pray about it. Sometimes God answers prayers not so much because we need something, but because we need to learn something. Even more to the point, Jesus told us, "Ask and it will be given to you; seek and you will find; knock and the door will be opened to you. For everyone who asks receives; he who seeks finds; and to him who knocks, the door will be opened."[5]

Is there something you desire, but you feel selfish praying for it? God knows about it anyway. Talk with Him. Maybe there's someone else who should hear your dream—or receive a plate of cherry macaroons from you! Only God knows!

We can ask for the desires of our heart, as long as we're willing to allow God to change those desires. Remember, He is the perfect gift giver. Pianos, trips to Israel, a spouse—all are blessings from God that also allow the receiver to give more generously to others. And that's all part of God's perfect plan—to bestow gifts that keep on giving!

Lord, I don't want to be selfish, yet I know, too, that I am Your child, the child of a loving Father who not only wants to meet my needs, but also wants to give me what's best. Help me to talk with You openly about my hopes and dreams, and, in the conversation, mold them to match Your desires for me. Amen.

CHAPTER 4

WILL GOD ALWAYS ANSWER?

There was given me a thorn in my flesh, a messenger of Satan, to torment me. Three times I pleaded with the Lord to take it away from me. But he said to me, "My grace is sufficient for you, for my power is made perfect in weakness." Therefore I will boast all the more gladly about my weaknesses, so that Christ's power may rest on me.

That is why, for Christ's sake, I delight in weaknesses, in insults, in hardships, in persecutions, in difficulties. For when I am weak, then I am strong.

2 CORINTHIANS 12:7–10

Dear Paul,

Some of my friends are always talking about how God answers all of their prayers. If I admitted that I have a whole list of unanswered prayers, they would tell me that I simply need more faith.

But I ran across that verse about the thorn in your flesh. God's answer was no, wasn't it? God didn't heal you, and you decided that was for the best.

But how did you know? Did you ever wonder whether you were making excuses for not being healed rather than admit your prayers were weak? I mean, wouldn't you have been better able to travel and preach if you'd been healed? I really struggle with this, because if God's answer isn't always yes, how do I know if I've been praying right?

When I consider my unanswered prayers, I wonder if I'm asking God for the wrong things or if God is making me strong by saying no. Did you ever wonder? After all, you were flogged, shipwrecked, stoned, beaten with rods, and thrown into prison. With all that happened to you, did you ever question if God was answering your prayers?

That reminds me of one other thing you wrote: "Do not be anxious about anything, but in everything, by prayer and petition, with thanksgiving, present your requests to God. And the peace of God, which transcends all understanding, will guard your hearts and your minds in Christ Jesus."[6]

Did God's peace guard you in all your hardships? Tell me, if God doesn't answer yes, how do I find that peace?

Prayer brings comfort, no matter how God answers. Ultimately, prayer isn't about finding answers as much as it's about finding a relationship with God. These next stories show how ordinary people found peace even as they wondered if God would answer their prayers.

For we are to lay our need before God in prayer
but not prescribe to God a measure, manner, time or place.
We must leave that to God, for he may wish to give it to us
in another, perhaps better, way than we think is best.

MARTIN LUTHER

Twirls of an Angel

NANCY JO SULLIVAN

When our children were young, our family always sat in the back row of church, ready to quickly whisk them out the door if need be. My husband held our two youngest children on his lap, while I kept a watchful eye on Sarah, our young Down's syndrome daughter. At the age of nine, Sarah loved church, especially the music. With curly brown hair and thick-lens glasses, Sarah smiled throughout each service.

One Sunday, when the organist began playing a lively rendition of "All Creatures of Our God and King," Sarah started tapping her feet. I reached for a hymnal, and in that instant, Sarah slipped into the main aisle of the church. While the entire congregation watched, Sarah made her way to the front and began to dance, twirling and swirling and bowing to the music.

I felt my face flush. "Not again," I whispered to my husband. For the last six Sundays, Sarah had danced in the church aisle when I wasn't looking. As her mother, I felt responsible for the disruption. "Aw, c'mon, let her dance," my husband said. He thought it was cute.

"Church is for worship," I reminded him firmly. I rushed to retrieve Sarah from the aisle.

Sunday after Sunday, as our family sat in the back row, I prayed, *Lord, please don't let Sarah dance.* God didn't answer my prayer. At the first opportunity, usually during the opening hymn, Sarah would sneak away from me and dance in the aisle, her arms waving like willowy wisps in the wind. "S-sorry, M-mom," Sarah would stutter as I escorted her back to our pew. "I-I-I…c-couldn't help it."

In the winter of that year, we enrolled Sarah in Sunday morning classes, which would prepare her to receive her First

Communion. "I-I-I…am s-so excited," Sarah said as I helped her find a place at a small desk in a basement classroom of the church. I looked around. All the other children in Sarah's class were nondisabled. *I hope no one teases her,* I told myself.

A young teacher with a ponytail drew near. I could tell she sensed my apprehension. "Sarah will be fine," she assured me.

I still felt uneasy. "Sarah likes to dance. She loves music. Sometimes she…."

The teacher interrupted. "Cool," she said in her perky voice, and then she firmly ushered me to the door.

After several weeks of preparation, Sarah was finally ready to receive her First Communion. On Easter Sunday, our family arrived at church a few minutes early. Sarah was wearing a lace dress with puffed sleeves; a long white veil completed her angelic look. She grinned as we took our places in a reserved front row.

Soon the church became crowded, and the ushers began setting up folding chairs. "I hope Sarah doesn't dance today," I whispered to my husband. On this special morning, many nonmembers had come to worship and celebrate with us.

The organist began playing the opening song, and Sarah started tapping her feet. "Today we welcome our First Communicants," the pastor proclaimed from the pulpit. "When I call your name, please come forward to be recognized."

The entire congregation focused on our front row when Sarah's name was called. Making her way toward the pastor, Sarah passed an elderly woman in a wheelchair and came to a halt. The lady smiled at her, and Sarah smiled back and curtsied.

Then as the organ music played on, Sarah made a couple of graceful glides and twirled her way toward the pastor, her veil billowing, her face beaming. I felt my face turn red. I rushed into the aisle to retrieve my child, but as I passed the woman in the wheelchair, she reached out for my hand. "Let her dance! She's just praising God." Her eyes sparkled with tears of joy.

I looked around the church. People were grinning from ear to ear. Some were even dabbing their eyes with tissues. I stood in the aisle and watched Sarah receive a certificate from the pastor, and then she twirled her way back to me. As the congregation applauded, God revealed His answer to my prayer. *Nancy, Sarah was meant to dance! This is her gift, her special way of worshiping Me.*

From somewhere in my memory, a verse from the Psalms surfaced, "Praise his name with dancing."7 That morning, Sarah taught me the meaning of those words.

After the service, I hugged Sarah tightly. "Mom, I-I-I am s-s-sorry f-for dancing. I-I-I c-couldn't help it," she said. I adjusted her veil so that my husband could take a picture of her, and I explained that some days were more special than others. "Today, it was okay to dance," I said.

With that, Sarah smiled and bowed like she was on stage.

"Sarah, stop dancing, honey. I've got to take a picture," my husband said as he checked the flash button on the camera.

"Aw, c'mon," I said. "Let her dance!"

Sarah is now seventeen. Over the years, she has taken dance lessons at a local studio and has a closet full of glittery dance costumes. She doesn't dance in church anymore, although she still swings her feet and sways to the music. Her custom dance routines are saved for Friday nights when she performs for her family in their basement recreation room.

Dinner's Under Control

JANE KISE

I inspected the dining room table one last time. Tablecloth neatly pressed, cloth napkins in place, silverware straight, salt and pepper bowls filled, and the butter out to soften. In less than two hours, my husband's parents would be joining us for dinner for the first time. Brian and I had been married just over a month, and I wanted to make a good impression.

Truth be told, my mother-in-law's gift for hospitality intimidated me. Her tables always sparkled with clever centerpieces and molded salads and place cards that gourmet magazines would have delighted in photographing. I'd even found myself praying about this little dinner party. *Lord, I know it's silly, but please let everything turn out okay. Joyce and Bob are used to the best.* I'd actually taken the day off work to get things ready.

I'd needed the whole day to clean the house and prepare, thanks to my complicated menu: roast beef with Yorkshire pudding, mixed greens with a homemade walnut dressing, steamed mixed vegetables, onion bread, and fresh pumpkin pie. Right up till five o'clock, I dashed between the vacuum cleaner and the mixer, forming dough into loaves and dusting the chandelier, straining pumpkin and shaking rugs. Finally, just an hour before Bob and Joyce were to arrive, I slipped the roast into the oven and headed to shower and dress.

A little after six, as I fussed with the napkins, I noticed that something was missing—the aroma of savory roast beef. I dashed to the kitchen, only to discover that I'd never turned on the oven. Just then, Brian walked in the door.

In tears, I explained. "We can't possibly eat before seven-thirty. How could I be so stupid?" I wasn't sure if God had ignored me or if He was trying to teach me a lesson about pride.

Brian said, "Mom and Dad are used to eating late, anyway. Let's just add some more appetizers to the cheese log. Let me help." We combed the cupboards and fridge for smoked oysters, chips and salsa, then sat down to wait for them.

Six-thirty came and went, then seven. They were *never* late. Brian even called to see if we'd messed up the date. Finally, just before seven-thirty, my in-laws burst through the door. "You won't believe this," Bob said, "but a gas tanker exploded on the bridge over the Mississippi. We've been stuck just a few cars behind it for the past ninety minutes."

Joyce had tears in her eyes. "We're so sorry. Is dinner ruined? You ate without us, didn't you?"

"No, no. Of course we waited," I said. "Sit down for a few moments and relax." I was tempted to hint that I knew how to hold a roast for an hour and a half, but as we sat down to a dinner cooked to perfection, I confessed to my side of the story. I joked, "I guess God knew when the oven needed to be turned on."

So I managed to serve the perfect dinner, but hardly because things were under my control. God showed His care for a nervous bride by helping things to turn out right, and in the process, I learned that God will always give me the answer I need!

The next time Jane invited her in-laws for dinner, the "fresh" produce she picked up the night before proved rotten at the core. In her nervousness over making the now sparse chow mein stretch to serve four, she accidentally added baking soda instead of cornstarch to the recipe (they're both in yellow boxes!). However, she's had plenty of time in the past twenty years to show that she really can cook—and to learn that the most important part of showing hospitality is the love that goes into it.

A Bouquet of Hope

NANCY JO SULLIVAN

I t was a snowy Christmas morning. The crowded church was decorated with fragrant pine trees and cherry red poinsettias trimmed with white lights. My family and I took some of the few remaining seats in the front row. While I brushed the powdery snow from my boots, I saw Linda and Joe slip into the pew across from ours.

Linda and I had been friends for years. I knew the last place she wanted to be today was in the front row with her sadness on display.

Over the past four years, she and her husband had been struggling with infertility. Time and time again she had assured herself that a pregnancy would eventually happen. Wishing for a baby had become a burdensome cycle of building up hope, then surrendering unfulfilled dreams.

A few weeks earlier, around Thanksgiving, it seemed as if their dreams would finally be realized. Linda and Joe had made preliminary arrangements to adopt a ten-month-old girl named Brianna.

It was to be an open adoption, so Linda and Joe's social worker had arranged for them to meet Brianna's young, unwed mother at a local restaurant. There, over a Coke, the birth mother assured them that she was ready to terminate her parental rights. "I want you to have my baby," she told Joe and Linda.

The next day, Brianna spent some time at Linda and Joe's home. For Linda, mothering Brianna felt so natural; everything seemed so right.

The early weeks of December passed quickly. Linda prepared for Brianna's arrival by buying diapers, baby clothes, and a little stuffed doll. She even monogrammed Brianna's name on a Christmas stocking.

"It already feels like she's my daughter," Linda told me one morning as we sat at her kitchen table.

But just one week before Christmas, and only one night before Linda and Joe were scheduled to become the legal guardians of Brianna, the social worker called with the news that the young mother had changed her mind.

Linda felt the all too familiar hopelessness as she hung up the phone.

Now as the church choir began singing the first verse of "Silent Night," I saw my friend wipe her eyes with the back of her hand.

After the service, Linda and I stood outside the church while our husbands scraped the snow from our cars.

"I feel like God is saying no," Linda said.

I reached for her mittened hands. "Maybe God isn't saying no," I said. "Maybe God is saying not yet."

A few days later I went to a floral shop seeking a gift of encouragement. A tall crystal vase filled with deep red roses caught my eye. The soft, perfectly formed petals overshadowed the thorns of the long leafy stems. It was refreshing to see something flowering in the middle of winter.

This is perfect, I thought, as the florist took down Linda's address.

"If roses can bloom in December, so can hope," I wrote on a small card.

When Linda received the bouquet, she called to thank me. "Sometimes it's hard to hold on to hope," she admitted.

The winter weeks slowly turned into spring. Linda dried the roses and placed one in her favorite book of devotional prayers. The couple continued to seek a child to adopt, and daily Linda fingered the brittle, dry rose in her devotional book and prayed, *Lord, increase my faith, sustain my hope.*

Then one morning, Linda and Joe received a phone call from

their social worker. "I have a young pregnant woman who is interested in you," the worker said.

Not long after the phone call, Linda dropped by my house. She was excited about the news, but hesitant.

"I *want* to have hope, but this feels so scary," Linda said.

I promised her my prayers.

Finally Joe and Linda received word that the birth mother was in labor. It was exactly one week before Christmas. Booking an early morning flight, Linda and Joe arrived at the Arizona hospital in the late afternoon, just a few hours after the teenager had given birth to a healthy baby girl.

After signing their part of the adoption papers, Linda and Joe watched the social worker knock on the birth mother's door; she still needed to give her final signature.

For nearly an hour, Linda and Joe paced outside the room.

Please, God, don't let her change her mind, Linda prayed. She couldn't help but remember last year's heartbreak of surrendered dreams.

At last the social worker opened the door and motioned the couple to join the birth mother and her new baby. "Everything is fine," the social worker whispered.

As Linda and Joe approached the bedside of the girl, they noticed how peaceful she looked. The teenager smiled tenderly. "She's always been your daughter." Then she gently placed her baby in Linda's arms like she was presenting a priceless treasure.

A strange mixture of sadness and joy washed over Linda. She felt compassion toward the mother as she imagined the grief of giving up her baby. At the same time she felt unspeakable joy as she cradled the infant she would forever call her own.

Groping for words, Linda quietly stroked the face of her new daughter. "You've given us an amazing gift," Linda told the mother.

A few days later, a beautifully wrapped package arrived on my snow-covered doorstep. Back inside my house, I pulled away layers of wrapping and found a dozen red roses arranged in a crystal vase. Attached was a message from Linda: "It's my turn to send the roses. This Christmas God sent me a beautiful bouquet...I'm holding her in my arms."

Joe and Linda's "Christmas Baby" is now two years old. They continue to believe that God orchestrated all the events of their child's adoption. Linda and Joe would like to adopt another child and are praying for God's guidance.

KEY:

Yes, No, Not yet, and I have a better plan
for you are all answers.

Anyone can see when God's answer to a prayer is "yes." It's harder to determine whether an answer is "no," "not yet," or "I have a better plan." As Søren Kierkegaard put it, "…life must be understood backward. But then one forgets the other clause—that it must be lived forward."[8]

One way to wait for the answer is to ask yourself, *Why?* Why might God's answer be no or not yet? Is there something you have to learn? Someone you need to forgive? What negative things might happen if the answer were yes? And what other answers are possible?

If God says no and answers the prayer in an unexpected way, what might happen? Might you just learn to dance, to delight in who God meant you to be?

Dear Lord, when I'm praying, it's hard to think of anything but the answers I hope to hear. I'm only human. I don't see all the things that You see. I forget to imagine what else You might have in mind for me. Let me be open to all the answers You might give so I can experience Your will for me. Amen.

CHAPTER 5

WHY CAN'T I PRAY MY CARES AWAY?

Near the cross of Jesus stood his mother.... When Jesus saw his mother there, and the disciple whom he loved standing nearby, he said to his mother, "Dear woman, here is your son," and to the disciple, "Here is your mother." From that time on, this disciple took her into his home.

JOHN 19:25–27

Dear John,

Whenever I visit someone I love in the hospital, or attend a funeral, or hear of the difficulties a friend is having with a child, I think of you, standing at the foot of the cross. How did you do it?

During your last night with Jesus, after you finished the Passover meal, He told you, "I have told you these things, so that in me you may have peace. In this world you will have trouble. But take heart! I have overcome the world."[9]

I imagine those words tore through your soul a few hours later as you stood in the shadows of the high priest's courtyard, watching that sham of a trial. The cobblestones and brick walls must have made the icy winds even more chilling that night. As the high priest struck the Messiah across the face, did you hope or think or pray that Jesus might call on God to rescue Him, to establish His kingdom then and there? Or did you take heart, assured that God would eventually overcome?

What thoughts filled your mind that day? Maybe some like these? This can't be happening. This is a nightmare! God, where are You? Jesus was right; life brings troubles, tragedies, and problems that seem to have no solutions. A Down's syndrome child may bring joy to our lives, but the disability doesn't go away. We're told the poor will always be among us. And eventually most of us face a final illness that prayers won't cure. When my life collides with these realities, I try to focus on God, but my passion for fairness and mercy screams for answers.

I confess that in the midst of trouble, I simply want it to go away. How can I grasp that God remains forever in charge, even in the midst of illness, betrayal, and all the other many problems that are a part of this life?

God never promised to fly us over the valley of the shadow of death, but instead He promises to walk with us through it. No matter what promises we claim, we will have troubles in this world. The people in the following stories found that God's promises are real and that prayers are powerful, even when the shadows of darkness surrounded them.

Unless we can look the darkest, blackest fact full in the face without damaging God's character, we do not yet know Him.

OSWALD CHAMBERS

A Time to Die

CAROLE PEARSON

My most powerful, compelling prayers were uttered when my husband, Jim, was diagnosed with lung cancer at the age of fifty-three. We followed all the recommendations for surgery, radiation, and chemotherapy. Friends, relatives, and our church family joined us in fervent prayers for his recovery. Finally his oncologist told me bluntly, "Your husband will die, but I don't know when."

I arranged hospice care at our home. Jim soon grew weaker, and his pain became harder to manage. I tried to act hopeful, but my actions gave me away. One day as I approached his bed, Jim said, "Each time you come near, you check to see if I'm breathing. You think I'm dying."

All the masks I'd been wearing fell away. It was time for honesty. I replied, "Yes, you're right. You are close to death." Somehow, my blunt words weren't unkind. I needed to say them, to acknowledge that these were our last moments together.

I helped Jim get a drink of water, while the words of Ecclesiastes echoed in my anguished heart. "A time to be born and a time to die…"[10] *Lord, I know Jim is going to die. But could I be there with him? That's all I ask now.*

It was a simple yet heartfelt prayer. After all, I didn't know if he would die within hours, days, or weeks. Even a half-hour trip to the grocery store became risky. Five times before, the hospice worker had been sure he was close to death. I'd been at the deathbeds of my parents, and I knew how that moment of death is so profound, so meaningful. I didn't want to be taking a shower or loading the washing machine. Even more, I didn't want Jim to die at a moment when our youngest son was alone in the house.

On May 7, 1994, my husband slept most of the day. My sons

joined me at their father's side at different times that afternoon and evening. Other nights I'd headed to bed for much-needed sleep, but this particular night I chose to stay by his side. Even though Jim slept on, I kept hold of his hand.

Around midnight I called the hospice nurse, "His hands are so very cold. What should I do?"

Quietly the nurse told me, "Either he's going into pneumonia or he's dying." She gave me a few brief instructions.

I settled my pillow and sheets on a sofa near his side. Periodically I got up to wipe his face with a washcloth and administer pain medication. Finally in the early morning hours, I fell asleep. When I awoke, on Mother's Day, I found that Jim had died. God had answered my prayer to the fullest. While I slept by his side, my husband slipped peacefully into the arms of the Savior.

God was with us through that season of death. I moved through the time to weep and mourn. Now my prayer is for "a time to laugh...a time to dance."[11] I think God is looking down and saying, "So be it; you are ready for a new season."

—⁂—

Since her husband's death, Carole's new seasons have included an early retirement and her last son moving out. Extra bedroom space has been converted into an art studio and a computer/writing room. The future holds time for art, writing, and travel, along with making new memories with family, friends, and those she has yet to meet.

Blessed with Car Troubles

RICK BYRON

Even though we live in the sprawling suburbs of Minneapolis, for years Sherrie and I had managed to get by on one car. No one would deny that we needed new wheels. Not only was the mileage on our old four-door fast approaching the two hundred thousand mark, but our third child would soon be born. Try as we might, three car seats simply didn't fit into the backseat. Besides, with church activities, grocery emergencies, and doctor visits, Sherrie needed transportation more often. Praying for the right car soon became part of our daily routine.

After weeks of praying, we finally found a used station wagon we could afford. I left the "new" car with Sherrie so she could celebrate her unaccustomed freedom. We laughed over her long list of errands before I sped off to work in the old beater.

Not three miles from home, the engine gave a huge bang, and a thick haze filled the air. I eased the limping vehicle to the side of the road, aware that my faithful car now sounded like a Sherman tank. All I could think was, *God, this is so unfair. This car has worked just fine all along with no signs of trouble. How can it give up on me so quickly? We waited, we were frugal, we persevered. Why can't we be a two-car family just for a bit—even for a day?*

Suddenly I had a much different thought. How had this old car kept going so *long?* Had God actually been answering my prayers for transportation? Images of a troupe of angels watching over us filled my mind. I could just imagine their past conversations. "Uh-oh, we're coming to a curve. You two grab the bumper, I'll watch the brakes, and the rest of you keep those pistons moving."

"Big hill ahead—everyone to the rear to push."

"We need two more angels over here to keep the windshield wipers working. And who can fill in for the heater?"

God had given us just what we needed, graciously allowing that old car to keep on working until we had new wheels. And we'd find a way to make do with one reliable car. I could almost see my flock of angels patting each other on the back as they flew on to their next assignment. I didn't need them anymore—at least not for another forty or fifty thousand miles—but perhaps that memory of them will help me recognize God at work a bit sooner the next time I think my prayers haven't been answered!

⊶———⊷

Rick and Sherrie ended up using their beater car for another year before giving the angels—and the repair shop—a rest. They are teaching their three daughters that recognizing God's blessings and protection in the midst of struggles leads us to trust Him even more.

Happy Birthday, Baby Jesus

Joanne Tarman

When I was a teenager, God gave me the desire to adopt a special-needs child. Nineteen years ago I brought Laura home. I willingly accepted her mental and physical disabilities. I even accepted the prognosis that she would not live beyond her teens due to her heart condition. I was confident that God would provide the strength and wisdom I needed to give her joy and fulfillment in life.

And, oh, the fun we've had! Usually Laura is such an example of God's joy. She awakes full of giggles and is constantly making up nicknames for people—I'm her "Blue Eyes."

Laura especially loves Christmas and all our traditions. On the day after Thanksgiving, we drink hot chocolate and listen to Christmas music as we put up the tree. Then we snuggle down in our sleeping bags in front of the fireplace and gaze at the lights on the tree. Laura falls asleep saying over and over, between giggles, "I'm so happy; I love my life!"

At least that's how it had been in the past. But this year there was no room for sleeping bags. Instead, a hospital bed stretched in front of our fireplace.

The night before Thanksgiving, when I awoke to Laura's call, the clock read 2:03. I stumbled down the hallway toward the living room, praying. *Lord, for once make it simple, like a drink of water.* But when I asked, "What do you need, honey?" my daughter's one-word response was, "Stomach."

I sat down on the edge of her hospital bed that filled our small living room. Quietly, I took her hand in mine. A year of endless tests had brought no end to her pain. The doctors couldn't find a problem, yet her misery was real. I'd finally rented the bed to make it easier for me to care for her. I couldn't squeeze it into her bedroom; it took the place meant for sleeping bags and hot chocolate.

With an elbow on her bed table, I propped my head in my other hand. There wasn't much else I could do until her pain faded. Perhaps outwardly I looked every bit the peaceful mother, but inside I silently screamed. *Lord, I trusted You to help me raise her. To see her suffering for so long—it's breaking my heart.* Where was the joy, the fulfillment in life, now that she couldn't even lie down to sleep? *Why, God? Don't You see her suffering? Haven't You heard our prayers for her healing? This is so unfair.*

Suddenly, Laura asked in a concerned voice, "Blue Eyes, where are we going to put the Christmas tree? My bed's in the way."

Christmas? I wanted no part of it, with all of its reminders of happier times. But I knew I couldn't tell Laura we were going to skip Christmas this year. Pointing across the room, I suggested, "Why don't we move that rocking chair and table to the lower level and put the tree by the stair railing? Then you can see it if you wake up at night." Laura giggled and clapped with excitement and relief.

Then she started to review all of our holiday traditions. "Thanksgiving dinner downstairs at Uncle Roger's. Friday put up tree, fire in the fireplace, hot chocolate, sleep out together. Christmas shopping. Christmas party at Grandma's house, 'allbody' be there."

I listened, amazed at how her focal points were the times with family and friends. Then she described Christmas: "Angels; barn; baby born; happy birthday, Baby Jesus!" She held her hands to her chest and exclaimed, "I love Jesus in my heart forever!"

I sat very still, chastened by my daughter who would never be more than four years old. So what if we had a hospital bed in the living room? Laura understood better than I did that God was here—He was here with us right now. Somehow we'd make it.

In the early hours of Christmas morning, I sat on the edge of Laura's bed, watching her sleep, stroking her hair, thinking of the lessons she'd taught me. I whispered, "Thank you, Lord," and Laura's eyes opened ever so slightly. A sweet, soft whisper echoed mine, "Happy birthday, Baby Jesus."

The hospital bed is still in the living room, but Joanne doesn't give it much thought anymore. She enjoys keeping a journal of the many "secrets" her daughter shares with her. To Laura, a "secret" is something that makes her day so special, she just can't keep it to herself. One day when her pain was so bad she couldn't get out of bed, she giggled as she whispered to Joanne, "I've got a secret! Look! The sun is out! " Whatever a day may bring, Joanne tries to listen for the "secrets" God wants to share with her.

KEY:

Prayer brings peace in the midst of life's storms.

There are circumstances that prayer cannot change. Nancy's Sarah is a twirling angel of a daughter, but she will always have Down's syndrome. Those who are scarred by the events of childhood can forgive and heal, but they can't change those events. When illness or betrayal or natural disasters threaten you or those you love, platitudes about living in a fallen world or about all things working together for good aren't very helpful.

Prayer, though, brings its own answers. In the midst of unchanging circumstances, prayer can bring God's peace and love. And those gifts from God can enable us to deal with life's storms.

When life hurts, picture those who seem close to God. The people whose stories you just read. The disciples, who watched as Jesus was betrayed and tried and crucified. Billy Graham, who suffers with Parkinson's disease. Corrie ten Boom, who spent months in a Nazi concentration camp. Horatio Spafford, who wrote the hymn "It Is Well with My Soul" after losing his four daughters in a shipwreck. They all found that God's promises are real, and that prayers are powerful, even in the midst of painful reality.

Lord, life can hurt so much, yet many of the hurts come in proportion to how much we love others. Love brings pain as well as blessings. That is reality. Help me to keep my eyes ever on You, cling to the promise that You are with me, and find the comfort that You alone offer. Amen.

CHAPTER 6

CAN I BOTHER GOD WITH THE SMALL STUFF?

On the third day a wedding took place at Cana in Galilee. Jesus' mother was there, and Jesus and his disciples had also been invited to the wedding. When the wine was gone, Jesus' mother said to him, "They have no more wine."

"Dear woman, why do you involve me?" Jesus replied. "My time has not yet come."

His mother said to the servants, "Do whatever he tells you."

Nearby stood six stone water jars, the kind used by the Jews for ceremonial washing, each holding from twenty to thirty gallons.

Jesus said to the servants, "Fill the jars with water"; so they filled them to the brim.

Then he told them, "Now draw some out and take it to the master of the banquet."

They did so, and the master of the banquet tasted the water that had been turned into wine. He did not realize where it had come from, though the servants who had drawn the water knew. Then he called the bridegroom aside and said, "Everyone brings out the choice wine first and then the cheaper wine after the guests have had too much to drink; but you have saved the best till now."

JOHN 2:1–10

Dear Mary,

Did Jesus have a twinkle in His eye when He told you, "My time has not yet come?" You knew Jesus was the Son of God; surely you struggled to know when you could ask for His help and when you needed to solve problems on your own. I know that I worry all the time about whether my prayers are bothersome to God, or if I'm truly bringing Him into every area of my life. Lost car keys, what to wear, what to make for dinner—should I pray about those things? I know the Bible says that we are to present our requests to God in everything, with thanksgiving, but I still wonder.

That's why I'm so glad you asked for Jesus' help at a wedding. Tensions run high even when a couple tries to keep things simple. Flowers, pictures, tuxedos, tiered cakes, ring bearers—so many chances for mishap. No, those things shouldn't matter as much as the bride and groom declaring their love for each other before God, but "small stuff" can easily become serious at a wedding! When those newlyweds tasted the new wine, surely they felt loved by God.

Is that how it felt to you? After that wedding, Jesus spent most of his time with His disciples, traveling and preaching. When you looked back, did the miracle of the wedding wine help you believe that your Son still cared very much about the details of your life?

While running out of wine would have embarrassed the bride-groom's family, life would have gone on. Gossip fades eventually. So why would Jesus bother with such a small matter? Because when God takes care of the details of our lives, we can experience God's love in a concrete way.

The following stories just might convince you to start praying for the small stuff.

❦

Some people think God does not like to be troubled
with our constant coming and asking.
The only way to trouble God is not to come at all.

D. L. MOODY

Only a Dog

ROBERT E. DINGMAN

I watched from our living room window as the neighborhood children and my four youngsters romped around in the front yard with our big dog, Rex. Did I say big? I mean *huge*. I smiled as our collie/husky mix threw my giggling youngest son to the ground, licked his face as if it were sugar, then took after another boy with equal vigor.

Great times always happened with Rex. This past winter, I'd harnessed him up to our sled, and he had effortlessly pulled it full of kids up and down the snow-covered street! He was both powerful and gentle. His only fault was his penchant for chasing cars and trucks.

The last couple of years had been tough for pets in our family. Someone in our rural town had been poisoning animals. We had lost two dogs and a cat and had known the pain of heartbreak, tears, and questions each time. So far, though, Rex, now three, seemed to have evaded the others' tragic endings. Our four kids—ages five to eleven—had truly bonded with this massive mound of fur. I breathed a prayer. *Lord, please keep Rex safe. We need him to stay around awhile.*

I shook my head and turned back to my accounting books for the family farm. I couldn't believe I was praying for a dog, of all things. *Get a grip, Bob. God doesn't have time for the small stuff.*

I believed in a powerful, just God, but it seemed only logical that God kept busy enough dealing with things that really mattered like war and cancer and the like.

The kids yelling at Rex suddenly interrupted my thoughts. I looked up to see him taking off after a passing truck. *Not again,* I thought, groaning as I got to my feet to call after him. Then to my horror, I heard a sickening yelp and watched helplessly as the truck's rear wheel suddenly snagged Rex. In one swift motion, his massive body flipped around like a rag doll with the rotation of the tire, before finally being crushed beneath the weight of the truck.

I ran out the door and down the steps to where the children had already gathered around their pet. His breathing was labored and unsteady; his back legs lay limp as his front legs pawed at the gravel. My heart sank. But my children were all on their knees surrounding Rex. Each had one hand on him, with the other raised toward heaven, as they prayed aloud for their beloved dog.

By then my wife, Pauline, came running around from the back. "Oh, Bob. Not Rex!" Her eyes searched mine for any news to allay her fears.

"Pauline, I don't know what we can do. I think I'm going to have to put him down."

"Oh, Daddy, no! You can't. We are praying, can't you see? Jesus is going to heal him." Russell, my oldest, looked at me with pleading eyes from his post beside Rex. I wanted to tell them, "Even people die in accidents. You can't expect God to save a dog," but I couldn't stop their prayers.

Pauline whispered to me, "Bob, I know it's an hour's drive, but let's have the vet take care of him. I don't want the kids to think you did it."

Pauline brought around our old gold station wagon, and I tried as gently as possible to pick up Rex. He looked at me with glazed eyes as he struggled for each breath. I placed him in the back where all four children could still reach a hand toward him.

The lengthy ride took forever, and my worries mounted. How were Pauline and I going to explain Rex's death to the kids? *God, help us know what to do and say so we don't destroy our children's faith.*

When we arrived at Dr. MacIntosh's office, he placed Rex on the cold stainless-steel table of his examination room. My kids stood back from the table as the doctor pressed his stethoscope here and there, poking and prodding. After a brief exam, the doctor looked up. "Well, Bob, he doesn't sound good. I'm going to need you to help me carefully lift him up by his hindquarters. If he can't breathe, his diaphragm is broken and there's nothing I can do."

The kids held a collective breath as Dr. MacIntosh and I lifted Rex, but the dog's eyes bulged and his lower jaw dropped as he gasped for air. We quickly laid him back down. The doctor shook his head. "I'm going to have to put him to sleep."

All four kids spoke at once. "No, Daddy!" "Don't let him!" "Jesus is going to heal him." "Please don't let him."

The doctor took my arm and guided me through the door and out of earshot while Pauline stayed and spoke with the children. I didn't envy her trying to explain.

"Bob, I see you've got a problem. Why don't we do this: I'll keep Rex here for the night. Sometimes there are powers greater than ours. If things don't improve, I'll just take care of him in the morning, okay?"

"That sounds good." I knew we were only delaying the inevitable.

Putting the children to bed that night was easy. They were all exhausted, as well as eager to continue praying for their absent companion. Pauline and I lay awake sleepless, trying hard to figure out how to handle the situation.

In the morning, Pauline poured herself a cup of coffee as I stirred cream and sugar into mine. All the kids were still sound asleep. Then the phone rang. Pauline and I looked at each other knowingly as I picked it up. "Hello?"

"Hi, Bob? This is Dr. MacIntosh."

"Yes?" I looked over to Pauline, signaling who it was with a nod.

"Well, Bob, I don't know what happened. Guess someone

heard those kids of yours, because your dog is up walking around. I examined him, and other than seeming a little stiff, I can't find a thing wrong with him. Do you want to come get him?"

What? I leaned against the kitchen counter and struggled to find my voice. "Uh, yes! I—I'll tell the kids. We'll be right there."

I hung up and told Pauline the doctor's words. Her shoulders dropped as she let out a big sigh. A smile filled her face. "Let's get the kids up," I said. "We need to tell them the good news."

I knew my children wouldn't be at all surprised. I'd spent the night worrying how I would explain things to them, only to have them teach me through the example of their simple faith. I knew that I would never forget that nothing is too small for God to notice—not even a pet dog.

⟞⟝

God touched not only Rex in a miraculous way, but Bob as well. Alhough Bob had believed in God for years, he had only heard of such miracles. "Seeing firsthand what God did for our dog and my family brought a new reality to my faith. It created a boldness in me that was never there before. I now want to let others know how real God is and how much He cares for us. Even in the little things."

Such Small Matters for Prayer

JOYCE K. ELLIS

When Steve returned home from the men's church retreat, my not-so-easily-excitable husband oozed excitement! As I washed the last of the pots and pans, I listened as he continued to voice his enthusiasm.

"It was a great weekend! You should see the campground. It's beautiful! Right on the lake. They have cozy little cabins and a huge recreation hall...."

Then Steve picked up a towel and began helping me dry the dishes. "But you know, something kind of funny happened."

"Oh?"

"We started each discussion period with about fifteen minutes of prayer. And Saturday morning Stanley had a special prayer request."[12]

I rolled my eyes. "Doesn't Stanley *always* have a prayer request?" Stanley was a fellow church member with a quirky personality. Small and skinny, Stanley wore a tie even on Saturdays. He often told anyone who was listening exactly what he thought God was saying.

Steve lifted one eyebrow. "He lost the stem for his watch Friday night, and he actually asked us to pray that he'd find it."

"Leave it to Stanley to make a big deal about such a little thing. How could he expect to find something so tiny at a huge campground?"

Steve nodded. "We were wondering the same thing. Nobody prayed about Stanley's watch stem during prayer time, and then, at the very end, Mr. Thornton stood. He sounded kind of emotional as he thanked the Lord for Stanley's prayer request and how it taught us that God cares about every little detail of our lives. Then he prayed that God would help Stanley find his watch stem and that each of us might be alert to help him look for it."

"Did he?" I asked.

"Did he what?"

"Did he find his watch stem?"

"Yes—just a few hours later. It changed everyone's attitude completely."

I looked at Steve incredulously. I felt so ashamed—ashamed at the smallness of my faith and ashamed of my attitude toward Stanley.

But it opened our eyes. Before, Steve and I went to the Lord with only the "big things"—crises and earth-shattering problems (at least to us). That habit was deeply ingrained in our characters. We had viewed the nitty-gritty stuff of life as things we had to handle. After the watch-stem incident, though, Steve and I began to see "little things" in our lives that we could talk over with God instead of worrying about them.

A few weeks later, we needed a baby-sitter for an important seminar we were supposed to attend. We usually hired one of the girls from church when we went out, but all the girls were attending the seminar. My mother, a reliable stand-in, was in the hospital at the time, so she wasn't an option. I strained my brain for days, trying to think of someone. Everyone was busy, and now it was the last minute.

We *finally* brought our request to the Lord. (Sometimes we're slow learners.) Indeed, the Lord cares about baby-sitting problems! A lovely Christian woman in our neighborhood, the grandmotherly type, volunteered to watch our children that day.

But what about even smaller things? I've been asking questions like, "Lord, what can I fix for dinner tonight that will make the most economical use of the food we have on hand?" Or, "Father, why is this talkative woman here at my door when I have so much to do? Show me Your purpose in causing our paths to cross."

I admit that I still take things into my own hands. Yet I'm

learning that things like frustration, dissatisfaction, and panic are symptoms of relying on myself instead of on God. Then I remember that watch stem. What a personal God we have—a great God who cares every second for every saint!

Joyce K. Ellis has published more than a dozen books, including *The 500 Hats of a Modern-Day Woman.* Joyce admits she occasionally prays for little things like open parking spaces, but as a freelance writer, she more often finds herself praying about her uncooperative computer, which can quickly turn into a big thing! The mother of three grown children and grandmother of two little ones, Joyce has learned that nothing is too small or too big to take to God in prayer.

The Lost Ring

JANE KISE

When my husband and I were first married, we attended a weekly Bible study. One Wednesday evening, we met at Rob and Jennie's, a sparsely furnished apartment with just a card table and a small TV that broadcast only one channel. They had gotten married just a few months earlier.

"Let's sit on the quilt," Jennie said. She and Rob motioned us toward a colorful patchwork they'd spread out on the living room floor.

Our group, ten in all, began to giggle as we huddled on the quilt, cross-legged. Rob passed around a plate of cookies. "Shall we sing 'Kumbayah'?" he joked. Jennie laughed and hugged her new husband. Though their possessions were few, it was obvious their love was strong.

For a good hour or two, we discussed the third chapter of 1 John.

We read the verse, "We have confidence before God and receive from him anything we ask, because we obey his commands and do what pleases him."[13]

"God cares about all our needs, even the smallest requests," someone said before telling a story of answered prayer. Soon others began relating similar powerful stories.

I gazed across the circle and saw Rob put his arm around his wife. I wondered why Jennie was wiping away a tear. She then told the group, "I lost my wedding ring. Can—can we pray that God will help me find it?"

Jennie went on to tell about the previous evening, when she and Rob had been watching TV and working on a crossword puzzle. "I took off my ring and set it on the quilt," Jennie said.

Rob sighed. "It just disappeared." They described how they'd turned the tiny apartment upside down searching for it. "There are so few places it could hide. Somehow it must have gone out with the trash."

Concern was mirrored on our faces. We all knew how special that ring was. Just after the wedding, when they joined our group, Jennie had giggled about not having furniture yet. Then she'd made a small flourish with her left hand, her eyes sparkling like the diamond surrounded by delicate filigree. "The only reason I have this beautiful ring is that it's an heirloom."

"My grandmother passed it down to us," Rob had added. "Otherwise, I don't know what Jennie would have on that finger!" It was obvious the ring represented the irreplaceable richness of their love.

Silence wrapped around us. Finally I said, "God cares about your ring." Everyone nodded. We joined hands and bowed our heads. "Lord, you love Jenny and Rob. Please let them find the ring."

By the time we left, Jennie felt better. "After all, it's only a ring," she said, but her chin quivered even as she tried to be brave.

That Sunday Jennie floated into the little library room where our group gathered, waving her left hand for everyone to see. There it was, her treasured ring, sparkling even in the fluorescent lighting. "You'll never guess where I found it the morning after we prayed—it's really a miracle!"

Jennie explained that she had awakened early and noticed that the quilt was covered with cookie crumbs. "I took it out onto our balcony, and I was going to give it a good shake."

Jennie paused to catch her breath; she was so excited to tell us what had happened. "Just before I flung the quilt over the railing, I saw something sparkling in the early morning sunlight."

Rob's eyes danced as he said, "It was the ring!"

Our group cheered. Jenny told us that the ring had fallen

through a small tear in the quilting. If she had shaken the quilt, the ring would have flown to the ground, three stories below, or disappeared inside the batting.

Rob and Jennie beamed at each other, then at us, as he squeezed her ringed hand. "Thanks for all of your prayers!"

It's been about twenty years since I've seen Jennie and Rob, but I think about them often. When I'm wondering whether or not to bother God with something small, I picture Jennie's joy that Sunday morning. If God helped a bride find a small ring in a patchwork quilt, then surely nothing is beneath God's notice.

⊙━✦━⊙

Since her children were born, Jane has met regularly with other mothers for prayer. Requests both big and small are offered to God—school friendships, sick gerbils, broken arms, and weeks at camp. Praying with others about those requests gives Jane the twofold joy of seeing God answer not only her prayers, but also the prayers of others.

KEY:

God is interested in the details of my life.

Of course, knowing that God cares about the details of our lives doesn't mean we should be irresponsible—should you keep asking God to find your car keys instead of finding a safe place for them? Or should you pray for a close parking space rather than accepting an inconvenient one as a God-given opportunity for exercise?

With that said, though, what *should* you be turning over to God? Specific prayers can be scary because they yield specific answers. You know for sure if God answers yes or no when you ask Him to help you find something. Sometimes general prayers such as "Lord, watch over us today" seem safer than "Lord, please help us find affordable snow boots for our kids."

That gives us two reasons to avoid specific prayers for the little things in life: doubts over whether we should bother God with the small stuff and fears over what the answer might be.

Rather than worry about the size of your request, focus on prayer as conversation with God. That focus does two things: It reminds us to listen, and it allows us to bring up anything in prayer. We aren't to fret about whether or not the subject is too mundane for God.

If you're worried about something, tell God.

If you tried solving something your way and it didn't work, take it to God. In fact, try to get in the habit of taking everything to God first.

If you can't remember something, ask God to remind you.

Of course, God's answer may be no, maybe, not yet, or I have a better plan, but the answer may also be yes!

Lord, praying specifically for little things can be frightening, since it will be easy to see whether You answer me or not. Yet I make huge requests like peace on earth without blinking an eye. Help me trust You, get to know You, walk with You daily by asking about things that seem small but will help me grow in my understanding of You. Amen.

CHAPTER 7

HOW DO I KNOW WHAT TO PRAY?

During the fourth watch of the night Jesus went out to them, walking on the lake. When the disciples saw him walking on the lake, they were terrified. "It's a ghost," they said, and cried out in fear.

But Jesus immediately said to them: "Take courage! It is I. Don't be afraid."

"Lord, if it's you," Peter replied, "tell me to come to you on the water."

"Come," he said.

Then Peter got down out of the boat, walked on the water and came toward Jesus. But when he saw the wind, he was afraid and, beginning to sink, cried out, "Lord, save me!"

Immediately Jesus reached out his hand and caught him. "You of little faith," he said, "why did you doubt?"

And when they climbed into the boat, the wind died down. Then those who were in the boat worshiped him, saying, "Truly you are the Son of God."

MATTHEW 14:25–33

Dear Peter,

I have a question: How did you ever get out of that boat? With the whitecaps crashing all around, how did you keep your balance to put even one foot over the side? Did the winds tear the wooden edge from your grasp, or did you willingly let go? I know you almost sank out of fear, but at least you were brave enough to try.

I have to admit that sometimes I'm even afraid to pray, let alone act. I know you'd tell me, "Just begin—God knows your thoughts anyway!" But I'm in the dark. Jesus was right in front of you. You could see what He wanted you to do. If I don't understand God's will, I don't know where to start.

What if I'm praying for courage to speak up in a meeting, but God wants me to keep silent? Or what if I want to be healed of something, but God wants me to learn to rejoice in all circumstances? Or what if I can't tell what is best in a situation?

I'm trying to learn from your example. Jesus must have made you feel safe, secure. After all, you kept getting out of the boat. Not that you walked on water again, but during your years with Jesus, you blurted out questions and thoughts that no one else seemed willing to voice.

You were the first to call Jesus the Messiah. You asked questions when you didn't understand a parable. That time you asked Jesus if forgiving someone seven times would be enough and He said, "No, seventy times seven!"—I think I might have stayed quiet after that, but you kept on. You made all kinds of mistakes, and even betrayed Jesus, but he still called you a rock, one others could depend on.

When I read those stories, I wonder what it was about Jesus that let you be yourself, while still becoming all Jesus wanted you to be. He seemed to draw you even closer to Him through your blunders. Yet, Peter, how do I know if I'm praying without thinking, praying without listening, or simply praying wrong?

Who knows, maybe the heavens laugh out loud at our concerns over praying correctly. Often, we second-guess ourselves when we just need to pray. Perhaps an aging parent is sick, or a friend's cancer has progressed so far that healing prayers seem less appropriate than prayers for comfort and release. How do we know?

Thankfully, God *does* know. Tell Him what's on your heart, as a small child would. And if you think you're straying a bit, remember Peter. God let him keep trying. In the next stories, you'll see how listening to God might help you know how to proceed.

*Unless self-will is voluntarily given up, even
God cannot move to answer prayer.*
CATHERINE MARSHALL

Thy Will Be Done

JOHN GATES

I sat in the hospital bed, feeling not like the husband and father I was, but more like a child counting on others to take care of me. I'd come all the way from Oregon to the Mayo Clinic in Minnesota, searching for answers that would free me from the seizures that had plagued me since I was a little boy. Most of my life, I had prayed for God to heal me, but now the doctors wanted to induce seizures, track down their cause, and evaluate the possibilities for surgery. My wife, Jen, sat beside me as technicians hooked me up to the machines and explained the procedures.

I squeezed Jen's hand and said, "I can't do this. I want God to heal me of seizures, not cause me to have them."

She looked at me. "Let God's will be done." Her words triggered thoughts about all the prayers that had been said for me on the journey that brought us to Mayo.

When I was thirteen months old, I fell off a porch, and a nail penetrated about three inches into my head. The X rays showed an air pocket in my brain that was badly infected. The doctors told my mom, "We've placed him in isolation. He has meningitis and a severe head wound. We give him only a slim chance for survival."

My mom sat in the waiting room and prayed, "God, I know you can heal. Heal my son!" Mom continued to plead with God on my behalf. Then she remembered how she'd given me to God the day of my dedication, and her prayers changed. "Lord, he's Your child. I want to see him grow up, but I know You love him even more, so whether he lives or dies, I will accept Your will." It was then that she relinquished all her rights as a mother and left me in God's hands. Immediately she was filled with peace. God began to comfort her by saying, "Let not your heart be troubled."

The next day, X rays revealed that the air pocket was gone. "We can't explain it," the doctors said. "We suggest that you allow us to take him in to surgery now so we can clean out the wound and remove any rust or hair that might have gotten inside his brain. The risks are extremely high. If he survives the surgery, he might be left brain damaged or paralyzed. Without the surgery, though," they emphasized, "your baby may again develop meningitis and even now might be immune to the antibiotics."

"Lord, let Your will be done," Mom again prayed. The surgery was a success, and six months later the doctors declared that I was completely healed.

Then on my fifth birthday, I had a seizure. The doctors decided the seizures were related to the nail injury. The seizures became more frequent as I grew older. Though I tried several different medications, nothing seemed to work. Mom tried to encourage me and kept reminding me, "God's hand is on you. He spared your life and has a plan for you."

Sometimes the seizures happened at school. It felt as if a very personal part of my life was on display. My classmates distanced themselves from me, as if they were afraid of me. Often I felt alone and self-conscious. "Can it really be God's will for me to live this way?" I would ask.

I began to ask God how He could use someone like me and why He chose to let me go through this. But my mom continued to remind me that God loved me, and I just needed to trust Him. I didn't understand.

Finally, in the eighth grade, God became real to me. Jesus had been pierced with nails, just like me. Jesus had died in place of me. It seemed natural to ask the members of our church to pray for me. In the worst way, I wanted to be free of seizures, yet it seemed that the more people prayed, the more seizures I had.

Slowly, I accepted the fact that this was how I would live. It became a part of my identity. Thirteen years passed with still no control over the seizures. I married Jen and became the father of a beautiful little girl.

New medications and treatments became available. None of them worked. The doctors told me, "After so many years of medication, you have less than a 2 percent chance of finding a medication that would work. Let's consider surgery."

Is it possible, God, that I could be healed through surgery? Jen and I prayed for answers.

That led us to the Mayo Clinic. Tests showed that the seizures weren't from the nail injury, but from a different part of my brain. Surgery would give me an 80 percent chance of being seizure-free. But there were risks. What should we pray for? Courage? Acceptance? Protection? Healing? Jen took my hand. "Let's pray for God's will," she said.

I bowed my head again, thinking of all the prayers said for me over the years. Jen was right; I didn't have to know what to pray for. I just needed to pray. *Lord, I'm in Your hands once again....*

An amazing peace came over me as I prayed. *I am a child of God. God* knows *what is best for me!*

Not only was the surgery successful, but I flew home just two days later. I'm grateful for the physical healing but even more appreciative that I have learned to trust in God, no matter what the circumstances. So many years ago, my mother learned the power of those words, "Thy kingdom come, Thy will be done."[14] Now, at twenty-seven, I understand, too.

Although inspired by the prayers of his mother, John says he would not be who he is today without the prayers and support of his family and friends. Since the surgery, John and Jen have begun to see God's plan and purpose for them. God used so many people to touch their lives during that time, and they hope to do the same for others. They lead a Bible study in their home and are now much bolder about sharing what God is capable of doing.

God Bless America

PHILIP S. BRAIN, JR.

Davao Penal Colony, a rice farm in the middle of the Philippine jungles, was home to a thousand American prisoners of war who survived the Bataan Death March. With the constant horrors of malaria, low rations, and sixteen-hour work details, how did these men keep their faith?

The rain thundered on the tin roof of my prison camp barracks; for twelve long hours there had been no letup. I lay shivering on my hard, wooden bunk, and I pulled a threadbare blanket around me. My fellow prisoners had been working in the rice fields since six that morning. I felt guilty as I glanced at the empty beds surrounding me, but I'd just been released from the prison hospital. Otherwise I, too, would have been working for hours in the wind and rain, standing in ankle-deep mud, clad only in a loincloth. I could picture the men with shriveled skin, blue lips and nostrils, and shivering bodies in the intense cold—bodies that had long before lost all their protective fat and suffered more and more as each minute wore on.

With my hands stiff from the damp chill, I smoothed the crumpled note that had been smuggled to me the night before. "Phil, I've just been operated on again. More bone off the leg. Would like to see you if you feel like coming. Walt."

Lord, what should I do, what can I say? I prayed, for I knew that Walt and the other men in the hospital were in danger. Our fellow prisoners were plotting to take over the camp. Some Filipino guerrilla soldiers, eager to fight back at the Japanese any way they could, had made contact with some of us as we worked in the rice fields. "We'll help you overthrow your captors," the guerrillas promised, "and you can hide with us in the jungle." The Japanese didn't guard us in the fields. Instead, they made us toil without clothing or food, reasoning that we couldn't escape then. But with the help of the guerrillas....

Only one thing had delayed the plan. If anyone escaped, the guards would kill the sick or wounded instantly. Even if we somehow protected them, we still wouldn't be able to carry all of them safely into the jungle. So we kept planning, hoping to find a way without sacrificing anyone. *Lord, we may all die if we stay here much longer, but how can we escape without bringing every man along? What should we do?*

I read the note once more. Walt and I had been in the prison hospital when I was recovering from malaria. The "hospital" was a nearby hut where men too sick to stand lay on damp, sagging cots. On one of my first days, I heard someone singing a Theta Delta Chi fraternity song. In the fog of fever, I turned toward the cot right next to me. My mind shot back to America, college, and the loyal friends I'd known. Homesickness washed over me, yet I felt suddenly comforted by the presence of a fraternity brother.

"I was Theta Delta Chi at Minnesota," I said weakly. "Name's Phil."

"Walt, Michigan," he answered. "Small world and all that."

That day, Walt and I did a lot of talking. We planned a great feast, conjuring up the warmest room imaginable. "We'll have prime rib and mashed potatoes and peas with tiny onions," Walt told me.

To pass the time, we tried to top each other's fraternity pranks—anything to forget where we were. Walt admitted, "We stole the clapper from the bell tower right before graduation. They couldn't toll the bells to start the ceremony!"

I laughed, yet I could see the stained bandages engulfing the lower part of Walt's leg. They had amputated his foot. And he was still singing.

A few days passed. Walt continued to receive treatment for his leg, but I got out of the hospital as soon as I could. Sick prisoners were given only half rations.

Now, staring at Walt's note, I knew that if I wanted to see him, I'd have to sneak back into the hospital that night. "Walt needs a friend," I told myself.

Again, I prayed. *Lord, what are we to do?* My prayers turned circles in my head. No outcome seemed right.

Around nine that night, I left the shelter of my barracks to see Walt. A dim light from the nearby mess shack lit my way. Between the low-hanging clouds and heavy sheets of rain, the Japanese guards couldn't see me creeping about.

The other prisoners were still out in the fields. Perhaps the Japanese knew something was afoot. Perhaps they'd increased our hours in the fields, hoping someone would crack and betray the plot.

With conditions so terrible, I wondered if some of the men might act on their own. I'd spent months in those fields with four hundred men, hungry, sick, and driven by bayonets to work. An escape might happen tonight.

I slipped into the hospital. Most of the men were asleep. I didn't have the heart to tell Walt about the plot. "Walt," I whispered, "the light was still on in the mess shack. The men assigned to the rice detail today are still out in the rice fields."

Weak as he was, Walt sparked with anger. "First they take away our food, water, and shoes so we won't escape out there. Then they work us worse than mules. But—" he grimaced with pain—"they can't break us."

We chatted a bit more, exchanging news about some of the other prisoners. Walt and I shook hands before I left. I wondered if I'd ever see him again.

I crept back toward the barracks. As I neared the mess hall, I heard a sound above the rain. I listened. My heart stopped beating for a second and then raced as it never had before. I realized I was hearing the diesel engine that pulled the flatcars the men rode back from the rice fields. But it was the sound of men yelling that had made my heart race. Their shouting rose above the noise of the train and the roar of the rain.

I was sure the prisoners on detail had overpowered the guards and were taking over the camp. *Lord, it's over. Be with Walt and all the others,* I prayed as I tried to decide which direction to run.

The light flashed on in the house of the Japanese commander as he ran out on the porch to investigate the commotion.

The train stopped about a hundred yards from the main gate. I could just barely see the shapes of men piling off, shouting even louder. I strained to listen with every bit of me, and the noise began to take form. Soon, tears mingled with the rain on my face. The men weren't shouting. They were *singing.* As they lined up in columns of four to march into the compound, the words of "God Bless America" floated through the air: "…through the night with the light from above…"

I relaxed and joined in the cheering as the men came through the barbed-wire gates. No one was going to escape; we were sticking together, a profound example of the brotherhood our country stood for. Walt wouldn't die tonight, and neither would I.

The next morning, the Japanese commander ordered all prisoners to line up. He then went up to the American commanding officer, saluted, and said, "I honor the spirit of the soldiers of Bataan." He pointed to the gate, where some of his men were bringing in wheelbarrows full of avocados and bananas and other tropical fruit. As we stood, waiting for our portion of his gift, I thought, *Walt was right, they couldn't break us, not with our faith in God and faith in America.* From that moment, I began believing I might live.

Even now, at the age of eighty-seven, the strains of "God Bless America" bring me to tears. I've never stopped talking to the God who stands beside us even in the darkest of times.

Walt also survived the war, and the two soldiers corresponded until Walt's death in the 1990s. Phil says that his years as a prisoner of war helped him to determine what was really important to him. He dedicated his life to service through a long career with the YMCA, where he met his wife, Delores, on his first day—she was his secretary. Phil spoke to civic and school groups about his war experiences until the age of eighty-seven, when his health started failing. Phil and Delores have two daughters and four grandchildren.

The Letter

DODIE DAVIS

I stared in disbelief at the letter in my hand. My son-in-law, Mike, had just informed me that I could never see my three granddaughters again.

My daughter, Kari, was only twenty-four, with two little girls and another on the way, when she was diagnosed with an inoperable brain tumor. Intense chemotherapy and radiation stopped its growth temporarily. But now, eight years later, Kari was dying as the tumor had spread into more brain cells.

At Mike and Kari's request, I moved in with the family the summer that Kari's symptoms worsened and her treatment resumed. I did a lot of mothering of the girls as Kari continued to weaken. I started noticing that Mike acted increasingly uneasy when I was around. I knew he was under terrible stress, but I sensed that he resented the close relationship between Kari and me, as well as my closeness to the girls. I was torn. How could I help and yet not interfere?

Kari spent the last six months of her life in a care center for terminally ill cancer patients. During that time Mike would not allow me to communicate with or see the girls at all. Many nights, I cried myself to sleep. I visited Kari often as she struggled to accept what was happening. I ached to comfort her little girls as well, as they watched their mother die.

Kari died two weeks before Thanksgiving. Now it was almost Christmas as I held Mike's letter in my hand. His words cut so sharply. *Lord,* I begged, *how can I bear not seeing Megan, Amanda, or Sarah again, when my heart is already crushed from losing Kari?*

That night I couldn't sleep. I paced the floor, asking God to give me something to hang on to, something to give me hope. A Bible verse I had learned long ago came to mind: "Cast all your anxiety on him because he cares for you."[15] This truth finally gave me enough peace of mind to fall asleep.

But the next morning, I plunged back into depression. What about Christmas? Would I be allowed to give the girls presents? Again the words ran through my mind, *Cast all your anxiety on him....*

I prayed, *Lord, You know all about this. I'm leaving the whole situation in Your hands. I'll wait and see what You will do.* I believed what I said, but a part of me still felt devastated and angry over the way Mike was lashing out at me. Was I the scapegoat for his pain and anger? And why me? I wanted to do something to show Mike how unfair he was being. I wanted to justify my position.

Lord, should I take him to court? I wondered. Weren't there laws about this sort of thing? *Lord, should I write a reply to his letter and sternly point out the verses in the Bible about how we are to treat each other as Christians?* But every time I thought about those things, I remembered that I had promised to trust God with the outcome. *Help me leave it in Your hands, Lord....*

Christmas drew closer and nothing happened. I wondered what the girls were thinking. Did they know about their father's letter, or did they think that Grandma didn't want to see them anymore? *Lord, help me let go. I can't control Mike anyway.*

Then one evening the phone rang. When I picked it up and said hello, a male voice said, "Hi...this is Mike."

My mouth felt dry as I tried to answer politely. "Yes?"

"I—I want to apologize for my behavior toward you," he said. "This wasn't your fault." He went on to say that he had been suspicious of me without reason. He had tried to make himself believe that I was stealing the girls' affection from him.

Then he paused. "I've tried to grow in my relationship with God while still hanging on to my anger against you. I haven't gotten anywhere."

My heart raced as Mike explained that Megan had confronted him about his attitude, saying, "When Amanda and I have a fight, you make us forgive each other. You have to forgive Grandma." He said that friends had been praying for him, counseling him against adding to the girls' grief by tearing them away from the love and support of their grandmother.

Mike ended our almost two-hour conversation by assuring me that I was free to have the girls at my house anytime. "And," he added, "when can you join us for Christmas?"

Just before hanging up, Mike said, "You know, I love you."

How easy it was for me to say, "Mike, I love you, too."

I hung up the phone and shouted, "Praise God!" My stumbling prayers had been enough. God was working all along, even when I didn't know what to do.

⁓⊱⊰⁓

After that Christmas, Mike arranged for the girls to spend one weekend a month with Dodie, so they could do "girl things." They get together for holidays, and Mike always calls to let Dodie know when school events are scheduled so she can attend the girls' concerts and plays. The family also took a trip together the following fall. Dodie continually thanks God for the ongoing role she enjoys in the lives of her granddaughters.

KEY:

God doesn't demand perfection in prayer.

Some people fall into the trap of thinking that they don't know the correct way to pray. The Bible tells us that prayer is easier than we think. Let's look at some examples from the Word.

When the disciples came to Jesus, saying, "Lord, teach us to pray," His answer was simple and brief. Most of us know it as the Lord's Prayer.[16]

Jesus honored a tax collector's simple prayer: "God, have mercy on me, a sinner."[17]

Jesus told us, "Do not keep on babbling like pagans, for they think they will be heard because of their many words."[18]

Jesus healed those who merely echoed the words of the Psalms, "Have mercy on me."[19]

Your prayers don't have to be perfect. They don't have to be original. They don't even have to be eloquent. You can simply come to God and say, *Lord, I don't know what to pray. Help me cast all my cares upon You and wait for Your answers.* All that truly matters is that you pray.

Lord, all my life I've tried to pray "right." Too often I've been afraid to open my mouth for fear of praying for the wrong thing or of using the wrong words. From now on, I want to come before You with confidence that Your Spirit will help me pray anytime about anything. Amen.

CHAPTER 8

How Long Must I Wait?

So David and Abishai went to the army by night, and there was Saul, lying asleep inside the camp with his spear stuck in the ground near his head. Abner and the soldiers were lying around him.

Abishai said to David, "Today God has delivered your enemy into your hands. Now let me pin him to the ground with one thrust of my spear; I won't strike him twice."

But David said to Abishai, "Don't destroy him! Who can lay a hand on the LORD'S anointed and be guiltless? As surely as the LORD lives," he said, "the LORD himself will strike him; either his time will come and he will die, or he will go into battle and perish. But the LORD forbid that I should lay a hand on the LORD'S anointed."

1 SAMUEL 26:7–11

Dear David,

When you found Saul that night, years had passed since God's prophet Samuel anointed you as the next king. You had no doubt that God meant for you to rule Israel even as Saul chased you through the desert, his obsession with hunting you down distracting him from his real responsibilities to his people. You were popular, you had an army, you could have won the support of many more. Did you ever wonder if God didn't mean for you to wait, but to take action for the good of Israel? Perhaps after a resounding defeat you could have negotiated taking the throne. Waiting so long must have been difficult.

Sometimes I am so sure I know what God wants, just like you knew you would be king. I'm thinking of times when I've prayed for healing in a marriage, or a new job for a friend out of work, or recovery for a stroke victim. Often the months stretch into years. Not only is it terribly difficult to wait, but also I start wondering if God was counting on me to do something besides pray. Or if somehow things are my fault and I need to seek forgiveness or learn a lesson before my prayers will be answered.

I've never been surrounded by enemy armies, but sometimes my circumstances seem nearly as frightening. And, like Saul's armies, they won't go away. How did you do it, David? How did you keep your eyes on God through all those years of waiting?

From a safe distance, David displayed the spear to Saul's army. Saul saw that David meant him no harm and called off the manhunt. But it was merely a temporary halt. Saul's jealousy and pursuit of David ended only with his own death in battle. What a challenge it must have been for David to wait on God's timing. The next stories come from people who found themselves surrounded by adversity, yet, like David, they kept their eyes on God.

Firmly and deliberately you say, "I do not understand what God is doing or even where God is, but I know that he is out to do me good." This is trust. This is how to wait.

RICHARD FOSTER

"Lord, Protect Her"

SUE TRAINIS

I collapsed into the pew at the back of the dark sanctuary, thankful to finally take a seat in the hallowed atmosphere of the small church. I was part of the leadership team for a three-day retreat. We'd spent the afternoon readying a presentation on Jesus' journey to the cross. Our makeshift stage was ready, I knew my lines, and the coolness that radiated from the brick walls called both my body and soul to rest.

My mind, however, was still going full tilt. As soon as I sat still, my thoughts at once turned to Carrie, my prodigal daughter, and the prayers the whole team had said for her at each meeting. This weekend she was finally coming home.

More than three years earlier, Carrie had fallen in love with Dan, a boy from her high school. At first Dan charmed us, too. He joined us for church services and helped in the kitchen whenever he came for dinner.

But then Carrie's grades started to slip. My daughter, who wouldn't venture to the grocery store without styling her hair, now seldom combed it or bothered with makeup anymore. Her gaunt face revealed weight loss, and she took to wearing baggy, unkempt clothes. Our long conversations over after-school snacks turned into fierce arguments. One day she slapped me in a fit of rage. I could no longer deny what I had suspected: Dan had introduced Carrie to a world of drugs we couldn't imagine.

Helplessly we watched as Dan and Carrie turned against us. We tried to seek treatment for her, but she denied everything. When Dan procured ski instructor jobs for both of them at a resort in Montana, Carrie leaped at the chance to get so far away from us. She was over eighteen; we couldn't keep her in Minnesota. I begged Carrie to take a cell phone, saying, "We'll come and get you if you ever need us." I feared for her life, literally, all winter long.

I looked at my watch. It was nearly seven. Carrie and Dan would be packing the last of their gear into the trailer they'd towed all the way to Montana behind Dan's truck. *Lord, protect her as they drive home,* I prayed. *Bring her back to us.*

But as I sent that prayer heavenward, a dank fog invaded my mind. A heavy feeling settled over me, causing me to sink deeper into the pew. Grief knotted my stomach with dizzying swiftness. I tried to take a deep breath to steady my suddenly racing pulse as frightening thoughts seared my brain: *Carrie is in danger. She may be killed. Pray—pray now!*

I jumped to my feet and scrambled through the pews to where Darla, my best friend, and six or seven other women were gathered. "Something's terribly wrong with Carrie. You've got to come and pray with me *now,*" I pleaded.

My face and voice must have conveyed the terror I felt, for they immediately followed me out of the sanctuary and down to the little room we had transformed into our prayer chapel for the weekend. There, in front of the altar, we sank to our knees and joined hands. I started praying. "Lord, I've waited all this time to get Carrie back. Please protect her.…"

I couldn't continue, but my friends took up my pleas. "Lord, keep her safe." "Jesus, we know Carrie is Your child." "Lord, we ask You to protect Carrie from whatever evil threatens her." "Bring Carrie home, Jesus. Help her to see Your love for her."

As they prayed, my heartbeats slowed and a warmth of calm lifted the weight from my being. Not even five minutes had passed since desperation had overwhelmed me in the sanctuary, yet now I felt equally overwhelmed by peace, the peace of God. I squeezed the hands of the women next to me and ended our prayer time. "Lord, I know You've heard our prayers. Thank You. Amen."

For the rest of the weekend, whenever Carrie came to my mind, that feeling of peace returned. I turned my focus from Carrie to the responsibilities I had for the retreat, feeling less concern for her than I had in months. I didn't worry even when Carrie called me and said, "We're having a bit of trouble with the trailer—nothing serious, but we have to take the back roads." So it would be six days instead of nineteen hours before she arrived. I knew she was safe. I knew she was coming home.

The morning they arrived, I heard the laboring engine of Dan's truck before I saw it. They'd parked in the street. I walked down the driveway, and at first I saw only the back end, crushed in and lights broken.

Then I saw the trailer, lopsided, pushed nearly off its wheelbase, the axles bent. "Carrie," I cried, "what…how?"

Carrie flew out of the truck and embraced me. Then she started to tell me what had happened the Friday before. She and Dan had started fighting while they packed the trailer, and they hadn't thought to balance the load. It had started to snow as they made their way down the winding mountain road. "There aren't any speed limits, Mom, and at first we were still yelling at each other. But it snowed harder and harder. I could tell the roads were slippery and asked Dan to slow down. He said that the brakes weren't working right and he was looking for a place to pull over when all of a sudden the truck jerked, then skidded. The trailer fishtailed—"

I interrupted. "When did all this happen?"

"Around six o'clock," she answered. *Seven our time,* I thought. *Right when we gathered to pray.* Carrie continued her story, how Dan had gone white with fear as he tried to gain control before they swung around a curve where there were no guardrails. The trailer slammed into the truck, then swung over toward the other side, catapulting the vehicle into a set of concrete barriers.

Stunned, Carrie and Dan climbed from the truck. They

learned later that the barriers hadn't been there the day before. The highway department had just placed them because of a recent accident when a car had plummeted into the valley below. Four men stopped to help. They jumped up and down on the hitch while Dan and Carrie pushed to swing the trailer around and out of the path of oncoming cars.

"After that we couldn't go faster than thirty miles an hour or the whole truck shook," Carrie finished.

I then told her about the terror that drove me to pray that Friday, and Carrie's eyes widened. "Do you really think God was with me?" she asked, her voice small and unsteady.

"Carrie, God will always love you, no matter what you do," I whispered, unable to talk past the lump in my throat. Arm in arm, we walked inside to her room, which I'd filled with helium balloons, pink, teal, and purple, to welcome her home.

I wish I could say that Carrie came home to stay, but in truth the next nine months were even darker than all the ones we had previously endured. Still bound to Dan in the intricate web of addictions, Carrie financed their drug habits by slowly draining the last of her savings with her cash card. The two of them disappeared for weeks at a time. One terrifying night she called home, sobbing, trying to tell us where she was, but the line went dead before she could finish. At one point the police actually searched for her body.

When despair threatened to overwhelm me, I clung to the feelings of peace I'd had in the church chapel, praying, *She's still your child, Lord.*

Finally, at three o'clock one snowy night, Carrie knocked at our door. Barefoot, coatless, her glasses broken, she told us, "I'm done. I'm home."

Looking back through all of the horror, I know that prayer and peace in the retreat chapel was God's gift to me, a sign that my hopes and prayers were not in vain. That night as I prayed,

Lord, she's Yours; bring her home again, I was convinced that Carrie was under God's protection. That gift kept me going until my little girl came home for good.

⌦—✦—⌫

Sue says that God's great power became even more tangible to her when she realized that she was able to pray for Dan's safety as well as for Carrie's. "God took away all the bitterness I'd had."

Carrie is now a flight attendant with a major airline. She says, "I know that all of the prayers my parents and their friends said for me made a difference."

Carrie was part of a flight crew from the East Coast on September 10, 2001. Several of the pilots and flight attendants on the next day's fateful flights were friends of hers. "Life continues to throw me curve balls. I rely on prayer every single day—I don't know how people handle life without it."

In the years following, Dan turned his life around, too. He worked with youth to keep them off drugs and had just been accepted into the navy's meteorology training program when he was killed in a tragic accident in May 2002. The verse used at both his baptism and burial was, "Blessed are the peacemakers: for they shall be called the children of God."[20] Dan had truly become a peacemaker.

Babies, Babies Everywhere

By Marlo Schalesky

Life conspired against me, crushing the wisps of hope I'd been foolish enough to nurture. Despite seemingly endless trips to the infertility clinic, I wasn't pregnant. Again. Still.

I wanted to forget about cradles and bibs, diapers and rattles, anything and everything that had to do with the baby I couldn't seem to have. So, with a tissue in one hand and the TV remote in the other, I plopped onto the couch to watch my favorite show. *Click, click.* There before me popped a cute, cooing baby whose mother told why Luvs were better than any other diaper. Quickly I switched the station. But there, a baby giggled at me from the center of a Michelin tire. My thumb pressed hard on the remote. *Entertainment Tonight* would be safe. I settled back into the couch as Mary Hart introduced a new John Travolta movie and…there in his arms was a smiling baby boy!

I shut off the TV and tossed the remote on the coffee table. Everywhere I went, there were happy parents enjoying their beautiful children. Mothers pushing restless toddlers in shopping carts, families gathered in church to pray, kids buzzing around playgrounds like a hundred brightly colored bees. I prayed, *Lord take this ache away…but what can fill it other than a baby?*

I needed a break, to escape the realities of infertility, even if just for a few hours. "Honey!" I called to my husband in the other room. "Get me out of here."

He peeked around the corner. "What's the matter? I thought you were watching that weepy angel show."

"Take me to dinner. Now."

Bryan raised an eyebrow. "What's up?"

I crumpled my tissue and threw it in the trash. "I've just got to get away from all these babies."

"Babies?" He glanced around the room, then looked at me as if I'd lost my mind. I told him what had happened.

He nodded. "A little Mexican food will cheer you up." And, forty-five minutes later, we pulled up in front of my favorite little Mexican restaurant. I glanced around at the empty parking lot and thought it looked like I'd get the quiet meal I needed.

Bryan helped me from the car, and we entered the restaurant hand in hand. I smiled and looked around me. Soon we were seated, and within minutes we'd ordered our favorite food. Gentle music drifted over the speakers. A candle flickered on the table. And best of all, we were the only customers in the whole restaurant.

Bryan cleared his throat, dumped a teaspoon of sugar into his iced tea, and stirred. Finally he glanced up at me. "You know, children aren't going to go away. You can't bury your sorrows in salsa every night."

I avoided his eyes. "I know," I said, as I dipped a tortilla chip into the salsa bowl.

Bryan stopped stirring. An awkward silence fell between us.

Finally I spoke. "The problem is, I don't know how to deal with it."

Bryan opened his mouth to respond but stopped as he watched the hostess lead another couple to a table directly across from us. "I can't believe it," Bryan said in a hoarse whisper. "Don't look now."

"Oh no," I sighed. There between the husband and wife was a brand-new baby nestled in a car seat. Just where I couldn't help but see it.

A sympathetic smile crossed Bryan's lips as his gaze returned to me. "Well, it's official," he murmured. "Looks like God wants you to face this head-on."

I grimaced. "But I don't want to." As I wondered how I could find joy in a world filled with children not my own, the baby's sharp cry broke through my thoughts.

I turned to see her little red face bunch up as another wail escaped her tiny mouth. Her mother looked as if she, too, were going to burst into tears. She whispered loudly, "I told you this would never work. We can't go anywhere anymore." Her voice sounded desperate.

Her husband scowled. "Is she hungry?"

"I *just* fed her."

"What about her diaper?"

"I changed it."

"Gas?"

"How am *I* supposed to know?"

With each exchange, their voices grew louder and so did the baby's cry. Finally the woman slammed down her menu, grabbed the car seat, and rushed toward the door. Her husband watched her go, then slowly shook his head and followed.

A full thirty seconds passed before Bryan spoke. "It's kind of sad, isn't it?"

I nodded. "It's downright absurd. You and I understand better than anyone what a miracle a child is. Yet people like that have no idea how blessed they are. That's more than sad."

"That's not exactly what I meant. I wasn't sad for *us*, but for *them*."

"What?!"

Bryan remained calm. "Don't you think it's sad that those people have a baby but they don't seem to be enjoying her, at least not right now? We should pray for them."

"Pray for *them?!*" My voice raised an octave as a hundred objections flew through my mind. I was the one who needed prayer. I was the one hurting. *I, I, I...* The pattern of my thoughts struck me. I was thinking of nothing but my own pain and loss.

What if I took Bryan's advice and prayed for the parents of

the children I saw? What if I prayed for the kids themselves? It couldn't hurt, and maybe it would help me, too.

"Okay, let's do it," I said.

He smiled, and I began forcing the words out: "Lord, please help those parents rely on you as they raise their baby. Let them enjoy every minute with her, even when she's crying. Strengthen them and give them wisdom in the days and years ahead. And bless the child, Lord."

A hand reached across the table to squeeze mine. "I think we've found your answer," Bryan said, "or at least part of it."

I managed a weak smile. "Maybe we have."

Since that day, every time I see a baby or a child, every time I feel the grief rising in my chest, I stop and offer a prayer for the parents and the child. Infertility still hurts, but it doesn't hurt quite as much. Maybe because it enables me, just for a moment, to see past my pain and into the heart of God. And that is a vision even more powerful than the sight of a precious child.

⊶⊷

Marlo still enjoys her chips and salsa at the Jardines de San Juan, but these days she's joined by one more person, her two-year-old daughter, Bethany! Marlo is also continuing her infertility treatments while working on her third novel. Her first two novels, *Cry Freedom* and *Freedom's Shadow* were recently released with Crossway Books.

Making Magic

RENAY POIRER

I tried to make myself comfortable on the small classroom chair, the only father at the volunteer meeting. My daughter's kindergarten teacher handed out sign-up lists. "Here are the various activities I need help with," she said.

"Could you tell me what's on it?" I asked. "I'm…visually impaired." Did she sigh or did I imagine it? I was sure I could read her thoughts: *How could you possibly volunteer in my classroom, then? Of what earthly use could you be?*

I couldn't really blame her. Since I'd lost my sight in an industrial accident three years before, in 1990, I hadn't been of much use to anyone. The doctors weren't sure why my sight hadn't returned after the accident. For the longest time, I wouldn't use the word *blind.* I often prayed, *Lord, let me see again.* But as months faded into years of darkness, I had to accept that I was visually impaired. I couldn't even change a light bulb, let alone continue my career as an electrician.

Besides my work, I lost my dreams of coaching my children's sports teams, of seeing my daughters, mere babies when I was blinded, all dressed up for dance recitals and birthdays and Christmas. I'd lost my independence, needing rides to go anywhere. I kept up my prayers for healing, but I couldn't sit still while I waited. I had to find work again to support my family. Vocational counselors suggested that I flip burgers or work in a battery factory, a far cry from the meaningful work I'd had.

Slowly, I looked into different kinds of rehabilitation. By learning to use a cane, I could stroll instead of shuffle, walk down a hallway instead of hugging a wall, detect a sidewalk crack instead of tripping on it. I started thinking of the cane as my magic wand, transforming me into an independent person once again.

Yet other people didn't view me that way. I still felt useless, a burden even to my own family. As the years wore on, my most constant prayer was, *Lord, help me be useful again. What can I do to help others that would be meaningful?*

That's why I attended the meeting to volunteer in my daughter's classroom. At first her teacher said she didn't have a place for me, but I pointed out, "I can listen to beginning readers as well as anyone." Reluctantly, she agreed.

I must have passed muster, for she began letting me chaperon children who needed bathroom breaks. I also could hand out papers for projects by standing in one place and letting the children come to me.

Glad as I was to be of some help, I still felt rather invisible, more of a prop in her classroom than someone who really contributed. Then one rainy morning, when none of us could go outside for recess, I asked the little boy who was reading to me, "What's that behind your ear?" and pulled out a quarter. Then I flipped it through my fingers and made it disappear. The "Wow!" that burst out of the little boy let me know I'd done it right.

That trick was one my Grandpa Meier had made us kids all practice until it was as easy as blinking. That set me to thinking: How many of Grandpa's other tricks could I still do?

Grandpa Meier worked hard to put a bit of magic into every visit we made to his house. Sometimes we three children—Randy, Rhonda, and I—crowded into the living room for a real magic show.

"Feel inside the hat, Randy. Are you sure it's empty? Okay, I'll wave my wand over the hat and—alakazam—Renay, what's in there?"

Even Mom laughed when I pulled out a stuffed bunny. Then Grandpa handed each of us a nickel. "Give them to Jocko. Put them right in his hand." Jocko, a toy monkey all dapper in top hat and red-and-white striped vest, always served as Grandpa's "lovely assistant."

Of course Jocko couldn't grasp the nickels, so Grandpa tried to catch them as they fell to the floor. Then with a flourish he stretched out his empty hands, wriggled his shirt cuffs, and leaned over toward Jocko, as if listening to him. "Hmmm. Rhonda, Jocko thinks one nickel hid itself under that book on the TV."

Rhonda said, "It couldn't get way over there, Grandpa," but got up and checked. And, of course, there it was. Randy's nickel had almost made it out the front door and was hiding under the rug. Years went by before I figured out that Grandpa planted those nickels around the room before we arrived.

Other times he had little experiments ready to go. Mixing dyes to make new colors. Building "volcanoes" with baking soda. Flipping glasses without spilling water.

I'd always planned on using Grandpa Meier's magic with my own children. He'd taught us all the disappearing coin tricks and how to use his top hat, but I'd lost my sight before I had a chance to try anything with Alea or Kara.

I called Grandpa Meier the night the kindergartner had so enjoyed my coin trick. Grandpa said, "You know what else would be easy for you? Remember how to keep cotton balls dry in a glass of water?"

Of course I did. Why had it taken me so long to remember Grandpa Meier's magic? The teacher gave me permission to show the whole class the next day. The children had such fun that the teacher suggested I come with a new idea each week.

Illusions and sleight of hand may seem childish to some, but for Grandpa Meier they were a way to be special to his fatherless grandkids (my dad had deserted us years before). For me, they were an avenue that helped children to see beyond my disabilities.

The hands-down favorite of the boys was playing football with me. I hadn't lost my throwing accuracy from my high school quarterbacking days; I just needed to know where my target was. The boys stood around me in a circle. They took turns calling out, and I'd pass it toward the voice. They never quite got over the magic of playing catch with a blind person.

I knew the teachers had grown comfortable with me when one day someone ran up to me in the midst of a recess game of catch. "All the teachers were having lunch," she said, laughing, "when someone looked out the window and said, 'Oh no, the blind guy's out there all alone with the kids!' It's hard to remember you really can't see!"

Grandpa Meier had a good chuckle at that one too.

Slowly, I started to feel like a contributing adult again. Perhaps I could find a useful career.

Shortly after Kara started kindergarten, I went back to school as well, to become a physical therapy assistant. School meant commuting from Wisconsin to Minnesota, learning the names of all the bones by feel, asking for help in transcribing notes, and so many other difficulties. Yet at my first internship, I knew God had answered my prayers to find meaningful work again. Without my sight, I had to listen hard to understand my patients' needs, and they seemed to know they could trust me. Often they even asked to pray with me as they realized that I, too, had a disability.

I used some of my schoolyard tricks with my patients. For example, I'd call a name, wait for the person to answer me, then walk toward the voice. Often the patients didn't realize I was blind until I asked them to help steer me down the hall. Their reaction? "Well, if you can do all this while you're blind, maybe I can get well, too!" Those words helped me believe that after years of darkness, I'd found a place for myself.

In 1993, Grandpa Meier's health deteriorated rapidly. I visited him as often as I could and regularly told him all the ways his tricks were helping me. I was able to be with him when he died.

After his funeral, my brother and I sat out on the porch of Grandpa's old farmhouse. Suddenly Randy exclaimed, "Oh, Renay, the northern lights are brighter than I've ever seen."

"I guess Grandpa's up there already," I quipped.

"Yep, doing magic tricks for the angels."

I didn't need to see the magic in the sky to say thanks to God for the magical light Grandpa Meier had added to my life, a light that helped me learn to believe in myself after years of darkness.

⚬━✦━⚬

Renay Poirer graduated from college in 1997 and went to work at a hospital in Eau Claire, Wisconsin, as a physical therapy assistant.

On May 23, 2000, while at work, Renay was nearly overcome with a piercing pain throughout his head. When he again opened his eyes, he could see the cross atop the hospital chapel through a window.

Doctors don't know why Renay's sight returned permanently after ten years of darkness, but Renay says, "The bigger miracle is that I learned to live again while I was still blind."

KEY:

Wait with hope; God is working.

Time goes so slowly when we're in a hospital waiting room. So quickly from the time a child first steps on a school bus to the day she graduates from high school. So slowly at the office if we dislike our work. So quickly when picnicking on a fine spring day.

Remember David? He knew he would be king, but those years of hiding and fleeing from Saul were a staggering test of David's faith. Many of the psalms attributed to David were penned during his exile, showing us that he concentrated on God's promises while he waited.

> But I trust in you, O LORD; I say, "You are my God."
> My times are in your hands;
> deliver me from my enemies and from those who pursue me.
> Let your face shine on your servant; save me in your unfailing love. (Psalm 31:14–16)

Yet David also wrote, "My God, my God, why have you forsaken me? Why are you so far from saving me?"[21] Do David's lamentations speak to your soul? Like David, you can pour out your heart's longings and fears. In the psalmist we have an example of one who praised, complained, and waited for God's answers. The key is he remained focused on God.

So in the midst of your laments and difficulties, always look to God. Are you missing any signs of God's leadings, such as an urgent call to prayer? Are you open to things you could be learning about yourself or about God? Are your eyes on God or just on your troubles? Trust makes all the difference when you are in a time of waiting. God has made everything beautiful in its time. (See Ecclesiastes 3:1)

Lord, how I hate to wait. Sometimes it's more than mere impatience. Sometimes the waiting is full of the anguish of watching someone I love suffer, or of not knowing if I'm doing what You want me to do. Please, Lord, help me know that You are with me, even in the most difficult moments of uncertainty. I trust in the wisdom of Your timing and Your answers. Amen.

CHAPTER 9

DO I DARE PRAY FOR A MIRACLE?

The night before Herod was to bring him to trial, Peter was sleeping between two soldiers, bound with two chains, and sentries stood guard at the entrance. Suddenly an angel of the Lord appeared and a light shone in the cell. He struck Peter on the side and woke him up. "Quick, get up!" he said, and the chains fell off Peter's wrists.

Then the angel said to him, "Put on your clothes and sandals." And Peter did so. "Wrap your cloak around you and follow me," the angel told him. Peter followed him out of the prison, but he had no idea that what the angel was doing was really happening; he thought he was seeing a vision....

He went to the house of Mary the mother of John, also called Mark, where many people had gathered and were praying. Peter knocked at the outer entrance, and a servant girl named Rhoda came to answer the door. When she recognized Peter's voice, she was so overjoyed she ran back without opening it and exclaimed, "Peter is at the door!"

"You're out of your mind," they told her. When she kept insisting that it was so, they said, "It must be his angel."

But Peter kept on knocking, and when they opened the door and saw him, they were astonished.

ACTS 12:6–9, 12–16

Dear Rhoda,

When you saw Peter, you believed that the miracle you'd all been praying for had really happened. No thoughts about ghosts or angels—you believed!

I picture you earlier that night, silently circling the room with bread and fruit for each guest, trying not to stare at the places where Peter and James usually sat. You had good enough reason to lose hope after King Herod put the apostle James to death. How all of you must have missed the booming voices of those two who had fished together long before they became fishers of men.

Several questions come to mind: Did seeing Peter at the door that night influence how you and the disciples prayed for miracles? Did any of you ever understand why Peter was spared, yet James had to die? I mean, why only one miracle when two were needed? Did you question whether you'd prayed hard enough for James?

Jesus told us, "I tell you the truth, if you have faith as small as a mustard seed, you can say to this mountain, 'Move from here to there' and it will move. Nothing will be impossible for you."[22] *Yet miracles don't always happen, just like with James. For example, our church prayed fervently one year for two tiny children with cancer. One lived, the other died. Did we fall short in faith?*

You were just an ordinary Christian like me, not a "super apostle." How did you pray after that night? I want to learn and be open to what God can do. Do you have any suggestions on how to pray for a miracle without losing faith if it doesn't come?

We can fall into the trap of the people interceding for Peter, praying in desperation for a miracle, then not believing it when it happens. Or we can be so busy looking for a big miracle that we miss the little ones God sends to strengthen our faith. Somewhere in between is a healthy expectancy that God can still move mountains. The next stories show what people learned when God showed up in unexpected ways.

Miracles are a retelling in small letters of the very same story which is written across the whole world in letters too large for some of us to see.

C. S. LEWIS

An Unexpected Lift

DAVID STARK

Being a youth pastor means you're a jack-of-all-trades. Travel agent, events coordinator, counselor, comedian, teacher, tour guide—I did it all.

One weekend I chartered an old yellow school bus, complete with driver, to take a busload of junior high kids on a camping trip in the mountains near La Jolla, California. I hoped and prayed that the trip would be a mountaintop experience for many of them. I'd planned a full schedule of fun—hiking, water games, relays, campfires, and, of course, times for God.

The bus bumped and lurched around curves of the twisting mountain road. Perhaps the lack of pavement added to the wilderness feel of the weekend, but it meant we traveled ever so slowly. I couldn't wait to get to the camp, where we could really start learning about God.

Suddenly the bus stopped. I heard the driver press down on the accelerator. The engine revved, but we didn't move. I walked up the aisle, noting the frown on his face. He said, "Let's go check it out. I think we're stuck in a rut."

We discovered that not one of the bus's tires touched the bottom of the ruts we were in. We were completely high centered, with the chassis of the bus resting on the high dirt mound that thousands of cars had created between the two tire tracks. Now what?

I made everyone get off the bus. A few of the boys were as big as I was. We tried to see if we could push. Nothing.

I had everyone get back on and pile to the back. Nothing. Then they all piled to the front. Nothing.

We worked for over an hour, looking for planks and then scratching at the sun-baked dirt. But never had a bus been so masterfully beached. It wasn't going anywhere. And neither were we, at least not in it.

There wasn't even a gas station for miles, but there were a few isolated homes in the hills. I decided we needed to send out a few scouting teams to get help. (This was in the days before cell phones!) But I thought to myself, *You'd better pray with them first. Their parents are going to ask if the pastor prayed.*

So to cover my bases, I had all the kids form a circle and join hands. The bus driver took part, too. "Lord," I prayed, "we're really in a fix. I know You've got a plan to help us out. Please keep us safe as we try—"

Baaam! A huge crack thundered through the air. I turned around and looked at the bus, thinking an axle must have snapped, but no, *the bus had moved. All the tires were now on solid ground.*

I'm not sure who was more shocked, the kids or me. I mean, I was just praying. I didn't expect anything to happen!

But more happened than just having our bus problem solved. Throughout the whole weekend, the kids were abuzz with a new excitement about God.

"Wow, do you think God reached down and picked the bus right up?"

"No, I had my eyes open—it was so cool!"

"We saw a miracle."

God used a bus, not my clever plans, to reach those junior highers. More kids turned over their lives to Christ that weekend than during any other event in my ministry. And all because of a bus. Perhaps we can't live on a steady diet of miracles, but a miracle or two can certainly open our eyes to the real might of the God we worship!

David, now a pastor, started looking for miracles after a trip to India, where people of faith seem more open to God's actions. Accompanying a worker across farm fields, David asked, "Isn't this king cobra country?"

The man replied, "Oh yes, but we just pray them off our grounds. We've never seen one." David believes that we could all use that kind of faith.

Healings

ALITA LAUGHLIN[23]

I cleared away the empty glasses and magazines from the night-stand in my brother's hospice room, making enough space to safely light the candle I'd brought. I hoped its delicate vanilla scent might mask the sickroom smells. Besides, candlelight seemed appropriate for this vigil, waiting for Jon to die of PCP, the pneumonia that takes so many people who have AIDS.

I'd spent much of the last week in this room with him. Jon's partner had died a few months before. I was the only family member who kept in touch with Jon after he admitted he was gay, so he really had no one else.

I closed my eyes to block the sight of his sunken cheeks and wasted body. How could this be the brother who had taught me to skip stones, who had taken the training wheels off my bike and run alongside me on that first spin around the block?

Well, it wouldn't be much longer, the doctors had told me. Jon's labored yet shallow breathing was slowing. I placed my hand over his, so thin and white, and tried praying one more time. *Lord, grant us…what? A peaceful good-bye? An end to Jon's suffering? After all, it's his fault—no, I don't mean that. He's my brother.…*

Yet that was exactly how the rest of my brothers felt, especially Bill, the oldest. He'd refused to attend family occasions with Jon if his partner came, and Jon refused to come without him. We hadn't had a family Christmas celebration in years.

Big brother Bill had been almost a superhero to Jon and me. He had let us tag along to baseball games with his friends, lobbing easy balls over home plate so we could get hits, too. Whenever I mentioned Bill's name, Jon's face still communicated the pain he felt at losing his big brother's respect.

An image snapped into my mind, a holiday photo card from

long ago: My brothers, decked out in red plaid shirts sewn by our mother, and me in a matching jumper, all huddled around Duffer, our golden retriever. Was Bill right? Had Jon taken all of that from us? I stared at the flickering flame, then at my brother. *God, help me. I am not my brother's judge.*

As I prayed, a wave of heat seemed to jolt my body, finally resting in my hands. They tingled with warmth. *Touch Jon; pray again,* I seemed to hear as a silent presence filled the room. Keeping one hand on his, I moved my other to his shoulder, almost withdrawing it at the feel of his emaciated, spent body. But as I grasped his shoulder firmly, words of prayer that I had struggled to find began to flow naturally. *Lord, be with Jon. Be with all of us. Somehow in his death, can we all draw closer to You...and to each other? Please help us.*

Suddenly, Jon gave a huge sigh. I thought he was gone, that I had just heard his last breath. But then his fingers grasped mine, and his eyes opened. "Hi-ya," he murmured as he stretched his other arm. "What a great nap, but I sure could use a sandwich."

Jon hadn't spoken or eaten for three days. I said I'd try to find him one, then I stumbled from the room to find a nurse or doctor.

So many thoughts competed for my attention. What had happened when I prayed? Was Jon possibly cured? Was this a second chance for my brother? Something remarkable had just happened, that much I knew.

The nurse took Jon's temperature and pulse. They were back to normal. By this time, Jon was sitting up, wolfing down a ham sandwich and asking for a chocolate malt. Later, test results showed his lungs were clear and his blood counts had improved. Although he definitely still had AIDS, the immediate danger from PCP had passed. The doctor was baffled; no one with the kind of damage he'd seen in Jon's lungs could have survived.

I called Bill and told him what had happened. After a

moment's silence he said very slowly, "Why were you even there? He deserved to die, the sooner the better."

Stunned, I said, "But he's your brother—"

"Not for years. You know that. He *is* dead, as far as I'm concerned."

"Well, apparently God doesn't think it's—"

"Maybe God doesn't want him, either."

I hung up, not knowing what to say.

The rest of the family had the same opinion, although they were quieter about it. They'd been relieved that Jon was dying, disappointed that he hadn't. My initial euphoria over the events of the evening dulled into worry. Bill and others had already hurt Jon so deeply.

Jon and I talked long and hard that night. "Part of me was ready to die," he said, "but I felt so empty, so incomplete. You know, I even dreamed that all of us were playing baseball again, yet I couldn't make it up to bat. This huge chasm opened between me and home plate, and I couldn't get over to the field to play with the rest of you."

I said, "If you sense there's even a crack between you and me, I want to fill it in."

"No, you've been honest with me for a long time." He grinned, "Thanks."

On the drive home I prayed, *So, God, why is he still alive? What is he to do with more days? What am I to do?* Slowly, a plan crept into my mind. But I didn't think it could possibly work. Surely it couldn't. Yet Jon was still alive, and that wasn't possible either. I knew I had to give my plan everything I had.

A few weeks later, my brothers each received a crimson envelope containing the picture of all of us with Duffer and an invitation to celebrate Christmas brunch at my home. I delivered the envelopes in person, holding on to the picture until I'd received their promise not to rip it into pieces. I said, "This picture is the truth. We're bound together. You can't cut Jon out without ruining the picture."

I won't say it was the best Christmas ever. We navigated through many awkward silences with the help of carols playing in the background and laughter punctuating the old home movies we viewed. But it was a start, a step toward healing.

A few weeks later, Jon called, a lilt in his voice, to let me know that Bill had invited him over to play cards, just as they had during college.

Jon lived another nine months, and in that time was reunited with every member of his family. The next time I lit a candle at the side of his hospice bed, Bill was there as well. Earlier Jon had told me, "I don't even mind dying. I don't want another miracle, for I received one bigger than my health. I never *ever* thought I'd have the love of all my brothers again. Thanks."

But I knew it wasn't due to me, any more than my hands had healed Jon months before. It was God who knew what Jon needed—the gift of time to rebuild our family.

—✦—

Alita shared this story at a spiritual gifts workshop taught by author Jane Kise. As Jane explained how difficult it is for us to understand when and how God chooses to heal, given that all of us eventually will die, Alita burst into tears and told the story of her brother's death, exclaiming, "Now I understand what God was doing."

Under the Shadow of His Wings

James F. Gauss

It was early fall, 1977. That year I had taken a position with the University of Illinois, and we'd just moved into a new home. Everything was looking good for our family after a long drought from good tidings.

Then Kathleen, my vivacious wife of fourteen years and the mother of our five young children, suddenly became deathly ill.

Kathleen rarely got sick, so when she first exhibited coldlike and then flulike symptoms, neither of us thought much about it. When our children were at school, she tried to get some extra rest. But within a couple of days, she felt more run-down and sought out the comfort of our bed much of the day.

One evening, a week after her first symptoms, she complained of severe aches and was too weak to get to the bathroom. I decided that it was time for me to take her to the hospital.

As soon as a nearby baby-sitter arrived, I helped Kathleen to the car and we drove the couple of miles to a local hospital. In the few short minutes it took, Kathleen grew weaker. I had to get a wheelchair to get her from the car to the emergency entrance. A doctor friend of ours quickly examined her. Obviously she was very sick, but he could not diagnose the root cause. Her blood count had dropped to half its normal level, the sign of a severe infection—but from what and where?

Kathleen was quickly admitted, then rushed to a room for tests and further examination. After a while, I was told to go home, get some rest, and come back in the morning.

The following day as I was getting our children ready for school, the phone rang. Nothing could have prepared me for the voice on the other end.

"Mr. Gauss?" the voice queried.

"Yes?"

"Mr. Gauss," the man said, very somberly and professionally, "This is Dr. Johnson at the hospital. Your wife is very sick. I—I don't think she is going to make it."

His words hit me like a ton of bricks. Thoughts whirred through my head, *No, no! No, Lord! How can this be? She only has the flu—she can't be that sick. Don't let her die, Lord!*

I don't think I even heard the rest of what the doctor said. All I could hear were his ominous words: *I don't think she is going to make it.* I tried to maintain my composure in front of the children.

"In fact, Mr. Gauss," the doctor continued, "if you had not brought her in last night when you did, she would be dead by now." He went on to say that they still hadn't pinpointed the cause of the systemic infection.

After I hung up, I choked back my tears and quickly pleaded with God to heal her body. *We can't lose her! The children and I love her so much. Please, Lord, please!*

Then I drove to the hospital to see Kathleen, praying that this would not be our last time together. She was on intravenous antibiotics, but so far her body hadn't responded. The infection seemed to have spread to every major organ. I would be allowed to see her briefly if I donned a mask, gown, and shoe coverings.

When I entered the room, I desperately tried to hold back my tears. Kathleen looked so pale, as if she were waiting for death's door to open. I can no longer remember our conversation, other than that we said, "I love you" over and over, assuring each other that somehow everything would be all right.

The doctors, though, were less optimistic. *"If* she makes it," they said, "she'll have permanent damage to her heart, liver, kidneys, and other organs." They had isolated a staph infection as the cause of her illness.

We who loved her simply couldn't accept that prognosis, so we began to pray, not just for her life, but for a complete healing. The small groups at our church gathered to pray, as did other friends.

During her first hours in the hospital, Kathleen was terrified of the dark, of falling asleep for fear she'd never wake up again. Yet just as she felt her fears nearly overwhelm her, she sensed a presence in the room, as if Jesus was sitting in the chair right beside her.

One night she awoke, startled to see a huge pair of wings enfolding her bed. From that night on she rested peacefully, assured of God's presence with her.

Within a few days, Kathleen started to improve, much to the doctors' surprise and delight. She was hospitalized for a total of five weeks. When she was discharged, she was given a complete bill of health—the doctors couldn't find the least bit of damage to any of her organs.

In addition to the gift of Kathleen's healing, God gave us a clearer understanding and appreciation for the many gifts we have, including our marriage, our family, and especially a relationship with our living and loving God. On September 7, 2001, we celebrated our thirty-eighth wedding anniversary, a precious time for us as we pondered the years we almost didn't have together. Every day since Kathleen was healed, even in the midst of momentary differences between us, we wrap our arms around each other, hold tight, kiss like childhood sweethearts, and say, "I love you." Whatever may come, our love is safe in the shelter of God's wings.

Although this was not James and Kathleen's first experience with God's healing touch, this miraculous answer to prayer inspired

them in the years since to freely pray for God's healing with anyone who asks. They have seen many miraculous healings in their
own family over the years and continue to pray for God's loving
touch, whether the need is large or small.

KEY:

God is still a miracle worker.

Of course, you could try to dismiss most miracle stories as mere coincidences. But can miracle and coincidence even occupy the same sentence? Is anything "accidental" with God?

Miraculous events change how the people involved think of God. Some may argue that they were mistaken, perhaps taken in by wishful thinking. However, others might argue back that perhaps people who don't look for miracles miss seeing God at work. Faith and miracles walk hand in hand.

Which is more miraculous, the healing of a person or a relationship? Both can seem hopeless, can't they? Yet God often uses events, timings, a letter, or a Christmas picture to work in His mysterious ways.

Perhaps miracles are tiny glimpses of heaven to remind us to keep our eyes on God. If you know people whose faith is particularly strong, you might want to ask them why they believe so intensely. Chances are, they might tell you of a miracle or two.

Lord, thank You for being the God of wonders, the God of miracles. Help me keep my eyes and heart open to all Your miracles, big and small. At the end of each day, let me pause to ponder what I saw and what I heard. Help me to always see You and Your hand in everything. Amen.

Chapter 10

How Can I Praise God When Life Hurts?

As they set out, Jehoshaphat stood and said, "Listen to me, Judah and people of Jerusalem! Have faith in the LORD your God and you will be upheld; have faith in his prophets and you will be successful."

After consulting the people, Jehoshaphat appointed men to sing to the LORD and to praise him for the splendor of his holiness as they went out at the head of the army, saying: "Give thanks to the LORD, for his love endures forever."

As they began to sing and praise, the LORD set ambushes against the men of Ammon and Moab and Mount Seir who were invading Judah, and they were defeated.

2 CHRONICLES 20:20–22

Dear Jehoshaphat,

Singing and praising…I know we're supposed to rejoice in the Lord always,[24] count it pure joy when we face trials,[25] sing praises to our Creator as long as we live,[26] and always give thanks to God.[27] But how did you actually manage to do that? With the armies of three countries just a day's march from Jerusalem, how did you manage to keep everyone focused on God?

Your troops shouted with joy and praised God, but I moan and groan on the way to the dentist or a contentious church meeting or a visit with someone who is ill. Yes, I pray, but it's usually, "God help me," not "Praise God." I know I should be thankful that I can see a dentist or that people care enough to attend the meeting, but my worries get in the way. And those are just little things.

What about circumstances that threaten to destroy us? When darkness and evil seem to have the upper hand? Not only do I struggle to remember prayers of praise, but I also wonder if praise might be hypocritical, especially if those around me are suffering.

Maybe if I'd been part of the crowd in front of Solomon's great temple the day before the battle, praise would come more easily. If I'd fasted with all the people in your kingdom, joined in your prayers for protection, then witnessed the prophet who leapt up, shouting that God was on your side, would I more firmly believe in the power of praise?

Or is the key once again deep inside my own will? Just as God let you know that you would win the battle, I can claim the promises that God is with me, that God's kingdom will triumph in the end, that evil has no control over my attitude or soul. Thanks be to God!

Whatever darkness or problem may threaten us, whether it is illness, family problems, job loss, or other circumstances that loom large enough to threaten to destroy us, we aren't alone. The following stories attest to how turning to God in praise brings light and life and hope. We know the end of the story; God is in control. No matter what happens, God is still worthy of praise.

Praise and thanksgiving do not magically change my circumstances. They radically alter my viewpoint.

JENNIFER KENNEDY DEAN

Thank God for the Fleas

ADAPTED FROM *THE HIDING PLACE*

CORRIE TEN BOOM WITH JOHN AND ELIZABETH SHERRILL

The ten Boom family had turned their simple home and watch shop into a haven for Jews trying to escape the sweeping terror of Nazi Germany. But they were betrayed. Corrie and Betsie ten Boom were thrown into Ravensbruck, a concentration camp. During their first night in the barracks, they discovered their straw mattresses were infested with fleas.

B etsie," Corrie cried, "the place is swarming with them. How can we live in such a place!"

"Show us. Show us how," Betsie said. It took Corrie a moment to realize her sister was praying. Then Betsie said excitedly, "He's given us the answer! Before we asked, as He always does! In the Bible this morning. Read that part again."

Corrie glanced down the long dim aisle to make sure no guard was in sight, then drew out her Bible. "First Thessalonians…'Rejoice always, pray constantly, give thanks in all circumstances; for this is the will of God in Christ Jesus—'"[28]

"That's it, Corrie! That's His answer. 'Give thanks in all circumstances!' We can start right now to thank God for every single thing about this barracks."

Corrie stared at her, then at the dark, foul-aired room. "Such as?" she asked.

"Such as being assigned here together."

Corrie bit her lip. "Oh yes, Lord Jesus!"

"Such as what you're holding in your hands."

Corrie looked down at the Bible. "Yes! Thank You, dear Lord, that there was no inspection when we entered here! Thank You for all the women here in this room who will meet You in these pages."

"Yes, and thank You that we are crowded," Betsie added, "that many more will hear Your word."

Betsie had to prod her sister before Corrie replied, "Oh, all right. Thank You for the jammed, crammed, stuffed, packed, suffocating crowds."

"Thank You," Betsie went on serenely, "for the fleas and for—"

The fleas! This was too much for Corrie. "Betsie, there's no way even God can make me grateful for a flea."

"'Give thanks in *all* circumstances,'" she quoted. "It doesn't say, 'In pleasant circumstances.' Fleas are part of this place where God has put us."

And so they stood between the bunks and gave thanks for fleas. But this time Corrie was sure that Betsie was wrong.

After each grueling day unloading boxcars and wheeling handcarts to a factory, and a dinner of thin turnip soup, Betsie and Corrie opened their Bible and spoke to any of their fellow prisoners who chose to gather. At first they huddled quietly, afraid the guards would discover their worship services, burn the Bible, and punish the sisters. But the guards never entered the central room of the barracks, even though at least half a dozen constantly patrolled just outside the windows.

One evening Corrie returned to the barracks late from a wood-gathering foray outside the walls. A light snow lay on the ground, and it was hard to find the sticks and twigs with which a small stove was kept going in each room. Betsie was waiting for her, as always, so that they could wait through the food line together. Her eyes were twinkling.

"You're looking extraordinarily pleased with yourself," Corrie told her.

"You know, we've never understood why we had so much

freedom in the big room," she said. "Well—I've found out."

That afternoon, she said, there'd been confusion in her knitting group about sock sizes and they'd asked the supervisor to come and settle it.

"But she wouldn't. She wouldn't step through the door. And you know why?" Betsie could not keep the triumph from her voice: "Because of the fleas! That's what she said, 'That place is crawling with fleas!'"

Corrie's mind rushed back to their first hour in the barracks. Silently, she again gave thanks to God for creatures she had seen no use for.

⌖

Betsie ten Boom died at Ravensbruck in December 1944. Corrie was released three days later. In 1959, Corrie visited the prison camp to honor Betsie and the ninety-six thousand other women who died at that camp. There Corrie learned that her own release had been the result of a clerical "error." One week later all women her age were taken to the gas chambers. She spent the rest of her life traveling to over sixty countries, spreading the news that Jesus can turn loss into glory.

Twenty-Nine Praises on a Crummy Day

JANE KISE

I distinctly remember leaving my early morning Bible study with four other young mothers, full of homemade rolls, great coffee, and a sense of God's peace. Energized, that's what I was, ready for whatever the day might bring.

By nine o'clock, though, I wondered if God was punishing me for being overconfident.

Mari, my eighteen-month-old, began her day by throwing a tantrum at the breakfast table, even though I'd served up pancakes, her favorite meal. Her cries were loud enough to wake three-year-old Danny.

At least Danny appreciated the pancakes. But while he happily sliced away at his cakes with the pizza cutter, Mari tripped over the blanket she was dragging around. The way she screamed, you'd have thought she'd landed on broken glass instead of padded carpet. I rocked and rocked her, finally sending Danny to fetch a book I could read to calm her down.

On my third time through *The Runaway Bunny*, Mari finally found her smile again. I caught a glimpse of my watch. It was too late to go to our play circle, one of my few chances for adult conversation during the month.

Danny was already hauling out our "road," pieces of green plastic track and bridges you can configure any which way. Danny generously gave Mari all the safe, smooth-edged cars, and we sat down to play.

Mari, however, wanted every car. She grabbed, yelled, "Mine!" and tried to push Danny away. I crawled over to help, but the instant I turned my back, Mari grabbed at a bridge, tearing apart the road. Danny looked at the string of pieces in her hand...and slugged her.

One, two, three.... I counted slowly before I reacted. After all, why wouldn't Danny be frustrated with his sister? *I* was! By now they were both crying. As I pulled them onto my lap, I caught a glimpse of my watch again. *Only eleven? Two more hours till nap time?*

One of the problems with parenting is that you do it on the fly. If I'd had even ninety seconds in a quiet room, I could have thought through the morning's events coherently. My normally sunny toddler crying over the least thing, fussing while we played with her favorite toy, quarreling and pushing? Something wasn't right.

Fortunately, Mari fell asleep before noon, allowing me to finally figure out that she wasn't feeling well—I decided she was coming down with an ear infection. Quickly, I phoned the doctor's office and was told there was a one o'clock appointment.

"But I'll have to wake her up...."

"Sorry, that's the last one we have."

So I took it. Furious at being awakened, Mari cried most of the way there. Both ears showed signs of infection. Poor child, she wouldn't swallow the gooey yellow medicine unless I pinned her arms and poured it down her throat while she screamed.

When my husband, Brian, came home from work that evening, Mari was already asleep for the night. "How convenient," Brian said. "She won't cry when you head to church tonight."

"Church? Oh right, that prayer class." I'd forgotten in the panic of the day that I'd signed up for a four-week class on prayer. "I think I'll skip it and put my feet up."

But Brian insisted. After all, I'd finished all the readings for it. Reluctantly, I changed into a clean sweater, grabbed my book, and drove to church, wondering if I'd be able to stay awake.

Our instructor asked us to take out our journals. "At the top of the page, write 'I am thankful for...' Then write down specific things that have happened that make you feel thankful. Stick with today. No generalities. You've got ten minutes."

Thankful for today? I'll be done in less than thirty seconds, I thought, thinking of all that had gone wrong. But, dutifully, I started my list. We *had* gotten the last afternoon appointment with the doctor. And Danny had been such an angel in the waiting room. Oh, and what if we'd gone to play circle with Mari as crabby as she was? And when she'd fallen asleep, I'd actually gotten dinner in the oven, with time left over to do a "big boy" art project with Danny.

My pen flew across the page: fun at bath time, being able to come tonight, that great morning coffee.... When our ten minutes were up, I had twenty-nine things I was truly thankful for. Twenty-nine things on a crummy day! Specific events, not the obvious generalities of family and friends, health and the weather. To include all of those, I'd have been writing through the night!

I finished with a prayer: *Dear God, I thought today was a disaster until I looked for Your hand in all that happened. If I'd kept You at the center of my heart all day long, I'd have been thankful instead of grumbling througout the day. How grateful I am that You care so much for us!*

c———⊁——o

Jane still keeps a journal of daily praises, counting her blessings before bringing anything else to God. Her children are now teenagers, and Jane finds that reviewing her old praise journals keeps fresh all the joys of parenting.

As the Waters Cover the Sea

NOËL PIPER

The early evening flight lifted toward the south into the dusky sky, departing from Beijing. I pressed my forehead against the window, peering downward to soak up my last sight of endless black velvet mountains rolling toward the horizon. From this altitude, their appearance of permanence and isolation and serenity was a different China than that of the pedestrians, bikers, cars, carts, smells, jostling, clamor, and solemn faces in the city I was leaving behind.

But not every face was brooding. Just a few days earlier, I had been sipping steamy green tea in a cluttered, concrete two-room cottage. Before biting into fresh figs from their tiny garden, I followed the example of my gray-haired host and hostess, using fingernails to remove the peel. As we ate, they told me the secret of their smiles.

One day, a few years earlier, they were trudging along the road to the next village. What used to be pavement was now pebbly fragments embedded in fine dirt. Every time a car passed or a rusty, crowded bus, the couple was forced over the jagged edge into the ditch. Even the bicycles of less poor travelers raised a red cloud that filled the walkers' eyes and lungs. After the powder settled, their lungs were still scratchy with the ever present coal dust, produced by the fires of every home, factory, and power plant in the province. A dark cloud covered them like the hopelessness of their lives.

In the distance they could see a group of four or five people plodding slowly toward them. A family? A group of acquaintances? Hard to tell yet, but they looked like every other person on the road—dusty, hunched under heavy bundles, and wearing shapeless, faded blue cotton pants and Mao jackets. Because it was unwise to pay attention to strangers, the couple studiously looked aside as they drew nearer.

But once within earshot, they were forced to stare. Filling the air was something they'd never heard on the road—or anywhere! Those ordinary-looking people were singing! And there was something not so ordinary about their faces. What was it? They weren't scowling. Their eyes seemed less...hopeless, was it? Was this what happiness might look like?

The couple dropped all pretense of disinterest. "People don't sing!" the man cried. "What are you doing? What makes you sing?"

"We are praising the true and glorious God, the King of the world," one of them replied.

My host and hostess smiled at me as they finished their tale. "Our lives changed that day," the woman said, "when we discovered that Jesus is the real God. It was the music that persuaded us. He had happiness to give away!"

Buckled into my window seat and still looking out over that ancient land, I thought of the millions of people who had never felt such joy...and how the simple sound of singing had beckoned my new friends to discover our Lord.

As the plane leveled out, I closed my eyes and breathed a prayer. *O God, please fill this whole land with Your glory as the waters cover the sea.*[29]

After a few moments, I lifted my head and looked once more out the window. My eyes were bombarded with gold, red, pink, and orange. It was like a new world below us. The mountains boiled with the fire of the setting sun, obscuring the line between the heavens and the earth. It was as if God were saying—shouting—"This land *is* filled with My glory."

Almost singing, I whispered a new prayer. "O Father of the heavenly lights, please open eyes to see Your glory surrounding them, so that millions more will sing the glory of Your name. And may I ever praise You so that others may see Your glory."

Noël was in China as part of a prayer team. Each day they walked in places of ministry and prayed over the days of Christian friends serving there. On Sunday, Noël attended the state-approved church in that city. From the balcony, Noël looked out over a dark blue sea of believers and sang "Amazing Grace" in English as the congregation sang in Chinese. She hopes there will be another China journey in her future.

KEY:

Praise lets me experience God's power and love.

How joyful are you? Could anyone gauge the joyful wonder of your faith by observing you? Chuck Swindoll once observed, "I've seen folks quote verses like 'Rejoice in the Lord always' while their faces look like they just buried a rich uncle who willed everything to his pregnant guinea pig. Something is missing."[30]

How different our lives can be when we decide that we will, as Paul decreed, "Be joyful always; pray continually; give thanks in all circumstances, for this is God's will for you in Christ Jesus."[31]

Remember Pollyanna, the heroine in Eleanor Porter's 1912 novel? Pollyanna's father, a minister, had told her, "If God took the trouble to tell us eight hundred times to be glad and rejoice, He must want us to do it." That's right, over eight hundred Bible passages tell us to "Be glad in the Lord," "Shout for joy," or "Rejoice in all circumstances."

Pollyanna "learned the secret of being content in any and every situation,"[32] just like the apostle Paul. Rejoice in the fleas, a nap for a sick child, and most of all, that God is with us even in the most difficult of circumstances.

Just being thankful—praising and rejoicing—is prayer. If life is hard right now, try writing down the things you have to be thankful for. If you just can't do it, head to the library for the original version of *Pollyanna*, the story of a young orphan, a girl without a home or a sympathetic ear or...well, we won't give it away. You'll be thankful for the laughter—and the truths about praise—it provides. Another idea is to spend some time writing down and posting some of those eight hundred verses about praise. And then be prepared to be amazed. An attitude of praise can change the bleakest of outlooks.

I praise You, Lord, and thank You for the many opportunities for praising You and how it changes me and my attitudes. May Your praise always be on my lips. Help me to look at life through the lens of praise and see all Your many blessings each day. Amen.

CHAPTER 11

IS GOD
ALWAYS WITH ME?

The LORD said, "I have indeed seen the misery of my people in Egypt. I have heard them crying out because of their slave drivers, and I am concerned about their suffering. So I have come down to rescue them from the hand of the Egyptians and to bring them up out of that land into a good and spacious land, a land flowing with milk and honey.... So now, go. I am sending you to Pharaoh to bring my people the Israelites out of Egypt."

But Moses said to God, "Who am I, that I should go to Pharaoh and bring the Israelites out of Egypt?"

And God said, "I will be with you."

EXODUS 3:7–8, 10–12

Dear Moses,

When regrets or fears plague me, I feel so alone. Trying to measure up to what God wants me to be seems futile. Is that how you felt? You didn't think anyone would believe you, or that you were eloquent enough, or that you were worthy of the task.

*Did your doubts come from regret over killing that Egyptian years before, when you fled the palace of Pharaoh, the only home you'd ever known? Maybe those regrets haunted you…*If I'd held my temper and worked for changes instead of killing the first time I saw someone beating a slave, could I have made a real difference? *Seeing the burning bush broke the peace you'd found in the desert, didn't it? Until that moment, it must have seemed a safe place, far from the courts of Egypt where you were wanted for murder, far from the other Hebrews who toiled as slaves, far from your past.*

So much of life is like that, isn't it? Regretting things in the past, wishing for courage to act in the present, dreading the unknown of the future. Perhaps what I face isn't as frightening as going to Pharaoh and demanding, "Let my people go!" But standing up for my values at work, or asking forgiveness for being unkind or judgmental, or facing my own death or that of someone I love, is just as overwhelming to me.

Your story gives me courage to pour out my own heart to God. Even though I'm not perfect, even though I make mistakes, even when my fears are stronger than my joys, God is still with me, just a prayer away.

As we pray, as we listen, as we change and discover answers, all that really matters is that God is with us. As the people in these stories discovered, our life here isn't all there is to the story. In the words of the psalmist,

> Where can I go from your Spirit?
> Where can I flee from your presence?
> If I go up to the heavens, you are there;
> if I make my bed in the depths, you are there.
> If I rise on the wings of the dawn,
> if I settle on the far side of the sea,
> even there your hand will guide me,
> your right hand will hold me fast.[33]

You have loved us first; if I rise at dawn and at the same second turn my soul toward You in prayer, You are there ahead of me, You have loved me first.

SØREN KIERKEGAARD

I Wasn't Alone

JANE KISE

Dad told us, "When I die, scatter my ashes over the Mississippi. I've always wanted to go to New Orleans." He knew that the mysterious liver and lung disease that had struck nine months before would claim his life. With all those weeks to visit Dad, to pour out my heart writing notes to him about special memories of my childhood, I really thought I was ready for his death. But I wasn't prepared for his dying.

That summer, my new, part-time consulting work helped me compensate for my husband Brian's crazy travel schedule. I took Danny, my toddler, to visit Dad as often as I could. Watching Danny hurl himself into "Bompa's" arms, whether Dad was sitting up or in bed, helped me adjust to his weakening condition. But as the summer wore on, Dad's energy waned rapidly. He went from taking walks around a local mall to walking down the block to walking around the living room.

The night our daughter, Mari, was born, Dad managed to make his way through the maze of hospital corridors to see her, but that was his last long walk. On the morning of Mari's baptism, he was too tired to go anywhere. A few days later, my mom called from the hospital. "It's pneumonia and peritonitis. They don't think he'll last the night."

I had to go alone; my husband stayed with the children. I let myself have a good cry before going to see Dad, so I wouldn't break down in front of him. *Lord*, I prayed, *if I start crying again, I won't be able to talk with him.*

Dad was hooked up to all kinds of machines, but he smiled when he saw me. I dug my fingernails into the palm of one hand while I held his in my other. "It was a tough night," he said. My prayers were answered; I was able to talk with him about the children and tell him, "I love you." I assumed I was saying good-bye for the last time.

Somehow, though, Dad rallied. We made plans to bring him home—with nursing assistance and maybe a big-screen TV for him to enjoy. On my next visit, we laughed over the newspaper comics and pictures of Danny raking leaves.

With a more positive prognosis, the doctors started a new treatment, but it failed. Dad's liver and kidneys stopped functioning. There wouldn't be another reprieve. His heart, though, was strong. His body somehow simply kept going.

Almost every night, Brian stayed with the children so I could visit Dad. He always rallied when he saw me, the twinkle sneaking back into his eyes, but the longer he lingered, the more difficult the visits became for me. Each time I prayed, *God, give me enough composure to get through this visit.*

During the third week of his hospital stay, I arrived one night as he lay gasping, trying to breathe. I stifled a sob as he mouthed the words, "I love you," before lapsing back into a semicoma.

I managed to sit a while with my mother, but I fled the hospital as quickly as I could. *Lord, how many times do You think I can say good-bye, not knowing which visit will be the last? I won't go back.*

You have to, God seemed to say.

But can't I just pray for him? I've said good-bye.

When you go—

God, I'm not going back!

I arrived home in time to read Danny's bedtime stories, but images of Dad's hospital room kept pushing aside everything else. *Lord, will he die tonight? You don't understand. So help me, I'm not strong enough to go back.*

I struggled to fall asleep that night, but in the early morning hours I awoke from a dream so vivid that I felt as if I'd seen it in a theater.

Dad opened his eyes. It was a beautiful, sunny day. No jacket, no sweater, yet he was warm in the bright sunshine. He got to his feet and filled his lungs, whole and healthy again, with the sweet air.

Close by was a path, and he started down it, gazing at the heather-clad hills. Soon he spotted Someone waiting for him by a bench that overlooked a panorama of lakes, mountains, and forest.

"I am so pleased to welcome you," said the Man as Dad drew near.

"Do You greet everyone this way?" asked Dad.

"Just those who came to know Me well during their lives, as you did. Although I'm sure you already feel at home, are there things you would like to know?"

"What about my wife?"

"I have already sent the Comforter to be with her. Besides, a love like the two of you shared doesn't end with life. You'll be with her in a thousand different ways over the next years."

"Will I be able to see my children and grandchildren as they grow? Can I help them?"

"You will remain a part of your loved ones on earth and will see many things through their eyes as they think of you. But as for helping them, you have already given them more help than you or they can realize.

"You taught them about Me, with your countless acts of service and compassion.

"You taught your children how to love through your devotion to your wife.

"You taught them how to work and to serve; they took your example to heart.

"You taught them how to laugh. They can chuckle at themselves and make others laugh, too.

"You taught them to believe in themselves, kindling a sense of self-worth that they are passing on to their children.

"You taught them how to leave this life behind, rejoicing in a full life, fuller than some would live if given twice as many years.

"You have given them a legacy they will cherish. It is your reward now to watch them grow and reap from the seeds that you sowed. Come now, there are many others waiting to welcome you to your Father's house. Well done, good and faithful servant."

At first I thought the dream meant that Dad had died; I even called the nurses' station to find out. But he was having a peaceful night. God seemed to say, *The dream was My gift. I am with you.*

The next morning I bundled up my baby girl to visit her grandpa, buoyed by the joy the dream had placed in my heart. God was with me; God would hold me as I visited with Dad.

This time, I savored the sparkle in Dad's eyes as Mari smiled and waved her little fingers at him. Instead of leaving exhausted and full of tears, I left with prayers of thanksgiving that God had allowed me to cherish the visit, which turned out to be my last.

A few days later, as I sat at my mother's side during Dad's memorial service, a few tears brimmed over, but I also smiled as I pictured Dad with Jesus. In trying to tell God what I needed—composure—I'd missed out on what God was trying to tell me, that I didn't have to do it alone. God was waiting to keep a promise, to walk with me in the valley of the shadow of death.

❦

Jane never forgot the lesson she learned from her father's death. When her cousin Jean was dying from breast cancer, Jane prayed, asking God not to make her go alone. Within the hour, one of Jane's brothers called, saying, "Let's visit Jean together. None of us should go alone."

Don't Ever Forget

NANCY JO SULLIVAN

I lay back in the dental chair, a huge wad of cotton in my mouth. The dentist had just yanked one of my upper molars, and he was in the next room writing me a prescription.

I'm glad that's over, I told myself.

Earlier that morning I had awakened in pain, my mouth throbbing from a toothache. I had to call several dentists before this one offered me an early appointment. Now from his tenth-floor office, I looked out on the skyline of department stores, restaurants, and hotels.

When my gaze fixed on a towering brick building labeled Ridges Medical Center, I suddenly thought of my older sister, Kathy. *Pray for her,* an inner voice instructed. I quickly dismissed the prompting. Just a week earlier, I had seen Kathy at a family picnic. We had spent the afternoon talking about the soccer games our kids had won, ideas we had for decorating our homes, and the new outfits we had bought at bargain prices. Kathy told me how excited she was to be teaching a Bible study at her church. Everything was fine.

Still, the inner voice persisted: *Kathy needs your prayers....*

I closed my eyes. Memories of my teenage years surfaced, and I saw myself at the age of sixteen. I was boarding a bus to Colorado, on my way to a Christian camp with my youth group. Before I climbed on the bus, Kathy handed me a Bible. "I want you to have this," she said. On the front page, she had written a simple message: "God loves you...don't ever forget that." That week God became a much bigger part of my life, and when I got back home, Kathy somehow knew that my faith had grown. "I'll be there for you," she told me. In the days that followed, my sister had guided me ever closer to God.

"Here's your prescription," the dentist said. "Try not to chew on that side." My pain forgotten, I grabbed the small slip of paper and headed for the elevator. I was already on my cell phone with my mother by the time the doors closed.

"Is Kathy okay?" I asked.

Mom sounded worried. "She's in the hospital. She's having a biopsy this morning. The doctors suspect cancer," she said.

I walked numbly through the lobby while Mom explained the seriousness of Kathy's condition.

"Which hospital?" I asked.

"Ridges. Ridges Hospital. Do you know where that is?"

Moments later, I stood in the hospital lobby. A gray-haired woman greeted me. "Your sister's being prepped for surgery," the receptionist said. "She can't have any visitors."

"May I write her a message?" I asked.

The woman smiled and handed me a sheet of hospital stationery and a silver pen. "I'll make sure your sister gets it before surgery," she said.

I began writing: "Dear Kathy, God sent me here. I have a message for you. God loves you...don't ever forget that."

For the rest of the day, I prayed for Kathy. Later that night, Kathy called my home. "I'm fine. Everything's benign," she said. She went on to explain how scared she was before the surgery. Right before she was wheeled into the operating room, someone handed her a note. "God loves you...don't ever forget that," Kathy said as she repeated my message from memory. "I read those words right before the anesthetic took hold." She was overcome with emotion as she told how much the note had meant.

I felt an indescribable appreciation for my sister. In our teenage years, she had offered me the gift of faith. Throughout the years, that gift has remained with me. Because of Kathy, I learned to listen to the still, small voice of God. Now, so many years later, God was still speaking to both of us. That morning, divine grace had brought the two of us together. I knew God would continue to use us in each other's life to remind us that He is always there.

⚬━✦━⚬

Kathy and Nancy continue to support one another as sisters in Christ. Nancy shares her faith as a Christian writer, and Kathy speaks often at local churches; their inspirational words offer hope and encouragement to a variety of audiences.

Though Darkness Surrounds

HELEN TURNER[34]

I didn't just adore my husband Len; I admired him deeply. As I watched him deal with congestive heart failure, he seemed almost superhuman to me. He managed to continue volunteer activities like recording audio books for the blind. He insisted that we still travel together. And every night until the very end, he asked me to kneel with him beside our bed to pray. "Thank You, Lord, that You are with me," he always began. His faith, he told me again and again, kept him going.

The twinkle stayed in Len's eyes even through those last weeks. Every time I saw that sparkle, I felt like God was with us. Len was only sixty-eight when he died; thirty-six years just wasn't enough time with this man that I adored and revered.

I felt like I was walking in darkness. My husband was gone; my children were grown. For the first time in my life, I was alone. Not wanting to wallow in self-pity, I threw myself back into my work as a family therapist. I loved my job and knew I was making a difference for the parents and children I worked with. I don't know how many hours a week I put in; it didn't matter.

But then I started suffering from shortness of breath. Even climbing up the basement steps after tossing in a load of laundry left me panting from the exertion. Rounds of tests revealed that I had obstructive pulmonary disease, a chronic condition.

Although the many medications had side effects and I had to get up at night for inhalation treatments, I was so thankful that I could still work. It was my clients' needs that kept me going. Eventually, I was even asked to apply for the executive director-ship of a small agency. At last I'd have a chance to build the kind of program I felt would be best. I couldn't think of a better way to spend the last few years I could work, leaving a legacy of sorts. I prayed that my health would hold out, that I could do it.

By that time, though, I used an oxygen tank daily. It couldn't have been more obvious that something was wrong with me. After learning of my illness, the agency withdrew its offer.

Losing the chance to run that agency crushed something deep inside me. I was as devastated as when Len first died. Yes, I could have fought them in court, but what was the point? They were right; who knew how long I'd be able to work? Not long before, knowing how much weaker I felt, I'd changed my prayers from, *Please heal my lungs,* to *Please just help me stabilize enough so that I can still be useful.*

But as the days wore on, bigger thoughts occupied my prayers. *Lord, how do I go on? Am I going to end up just being a burden to my kids? What good am I to You if I can't work anymore?* My answer back from God? Nothing. It was as if I were trying to phone God and couldn't even get a dial tone.

I still knelt every night to pray, but I couldn't find the peace Len had spoken of and demonstrated. *God, please show me the light of Your love so I can keep going,* I pleaded. But instead of peace, the sermons I'd heard all through my childhood kept flooding back. *We're all terrible sinners, but if we do everything right our whole lives, just maybe we might slip into heaven.* Intellectually, I knew my illness wasn't a punishment for my sins, but emotionally I felt that God simply didn't love me. Now I wasn't even useful. How could I do anything for God?

When severe breathing problems led to repeated hospitalizations, I learned that my heart was failing as well. The doctor's advice? "Get your affairs in order."

With more urgency than ever, I threw myself into everything I could manage at church, still waiting to hear from God. I manned an information table on Sunday mornings, I led a couple of small groups, I attended adult Sunday school classes, and I met with my pastor. He told me, "God *is* with you. Keep praying for peace, and know I'll be praying that you find it."

Some days I managed to still my thoughts and focus on being thankful for all the things I could still do. I could still read stories to my grandchildren, still drive a car the few blocks to church, still live in my own home.

But at night, as I struggled to breathe, to sleep, to even lie still long enough to doze off, once again darkness clutched at my mind as my fears for the future blotted out everything else. The hum of the oxygen tank echoed through my bedroom, as cold and dark as my thoughts. Often I drifted off for only an hour at a time of restless dreaming, where my fears again caught up with me.

One night I stayed up late reading, hoping that would help me sleep a bit longer. I must have nodded off, for I suddenly felt peaceful, as if bathed in a warmth I hadn't known before. I opened my eyes, thinking I might as well get a drink of water, and thought, *Why is it so bright in here? I know it's still nighttime.*

The room glowed with a golden light, yet my alarm clock read three o'clock. There weren't any shadows anywhere. Instead, the air almost shivered with iridescence, like the glow of a perfect sunset transforming the horizon. I stared toward the windows, then the door, and I felt a presence I can only describe as love.

The next thing I knew, it was morning. I had actually slept for several hours. I lay still for a moment and thought about the beautiful dream of light I'd had. Yes, it was just a dream, but it was such a contrast to my mood of the night before that I knew somehow it was from God. I knew God was telling me I wasn't alone.

With that thought it was a bit easier to get up that morning, to brew coffee for just one person, to treat myself to scrambled eggs instead of a bowl of cold cereal. As I sat down to eat, the phone rang.

"Helen?" It was my neighbor's voice. "I just had to see if you were okay this morning."

"Yes, I'm fine. Why?" I answered.

"Well, when I got up in the middle of the night for a glass of water, I saw that every light in your house was on. I watched for an ambulance or something, but then the lights went out again, so I assumed you were all right."

"Why, thanks; yes, I am," I repeated. I hung up the phone and had to sit down, fast. It hadn't been a dream after all! God had visited my room.

For the rest of the morning, I flitted from one thing to the next as my heart sang the refrain: *God loves me!* Yet why me? Why had God done something so wonderful for doubting, faithless me?

Then I remembered something our pastor had said in a sermon: "God wants every one of you in heaven. God loves you and wants to find you." *That* was the peace, the joy my husband had spoken of. I felt humbled, unworthy, yet exhilarated.

I'd prayed for a miracle and I got one: discovering the joy of being a child of God. No, my health hasn't improved. I've had to stop working altogether. Yet even during my worst nights, I can now see the twinkle in my husband's eye and feel the light that once filled this room. I *know* God is with me.

⌒—⋈—⌒

The author of this story asked that her name be changed because, "My friends all see me as so down-to-earth. They wouldn't believe this really happened!" But she wants others to know that in praying for a miracle, she received something better—the joy of knowing that God loves her and will always be with her.

KEY:

God will never desert me.

No one walks through life unscathed, yet not one of us has to walk alone.

Think of St. Thérèse of Lisieux, dying of tuberculosis at the age of twenty-four, telling her sisters in Christ, "I have really taken to heart the words of Job, *'Even if God should kill me I would still trust in Him.' (Job 13:15)* My heart is filled to the brim with the will of our Lord so that nothing else can find place there, but glides across like oil over tranquil waters."[35]

Think of Dietrich Bonhoeffer, who penned in one of his last letters from a Nazi prison, "I am so sure of God's guiding hand that I hope I shall always be kept in that certainty. You must never doubt that I'm traveling with gratitude and cheerfulness along the road where I'm being led. My past life is brim-full of God's goodness, and my sins are covered by the forgiving love of Christ crucified."[36]

Think of Martin Luther King, Jr. crying the night before he was assassinated, "Like anybody, I would like to live a long life…but I'm not concerned about that now, I just want to do God's will. And He's allowed me to go up to the mountain…I'm not worried about anything."[37]

Think of Jesus in the Garden of Gethsemane, pleading to escape death on the cross, yet finally saying, "Not my will, but thine, be done.…"[38]

Let the words of the apostle Paul assure you of the nearness of God:

For I am convinced that neither death nor life,
neither angels nor demons,
neither the present nor the future, nor any powers,

neither height nor depth, nor anything else in all creation,
will be able to separate us from the love of God that is in Christ Jesus our Lord.[39]

You are never alone. Never abandoned. God is with you today, tomorrow, and forever.

Lord, help me to know Your presence, even in the moments when You seem far away or when I can't seem to find You at all. No matter what I do or what happens in my life, let me remember that You love me always and will be with me forever. Amen.

The publisher and author would love to hear your comments about this book. *Please contact us at:* www.whenwepray.com

NOTES

1. 2 Corinthians 12:9
2. Revelation 3:20, NKJV
3. Psalm 139:4
4. Ezekiel 3:4–5
5. Luke 11:9–10
6. Philippians 4:6–7
7. Psalm 149:3
8. Søren Kierkegaard, *Journals and Papers [1843], vol. I* as quoted by Justin Kaplan, ed., *Bartlett's Familiar Quotations,* 16th ed. (New York: Little Brown, 1992) 473.
9. John 16:33
10. Ecclesiastes 3:2
11. Ecclesiastes 3:4
12. Names and some details have been changed.
13. 1 John 3:21–22
14. Matthew 6:10, KJV
15. 1 Peter 5:7
16. Luke 11:1–4
17. Luke 18:13
18. Matthew 6:7
19. Psalm 51:1; Luke 18:38
20. Matthew 5:9, KJV
21. Psalm 22:1
22. Matthew 17:20
23. Names and details have been changed.
24. Philippians 4:4
25. James 1:2
26. Psalm 146:2
27. Ephesians 5:20

28. 1 Thessalonians 5:16-18, RSV

29. Habakkuk 2:14

30. Chuck Swindoll, *Laugh Again* (Dallas: Word Publishing, 1992) 243.

31. 1 Thessalonians 5:16–18

32. Philippians 4:12

33. Psalm 139:7–10

34. Name has been changed.

35. St. Thérèse of Lisieux, *The Story of a Soul* (New York: Book-of-the-Month Club, 1996), 213.

36. Dietrich Bonhoeffer, *Letters and Papers from Prison*, ed. Eberhard Bethge (New York: Collier Books, 1971), 393.

37. Martin Luther King, Jr., address to sanitation workers, Memphis, Tennessee [April 3, 1968] as quoted by Justin Kaplan, ed., *Bartlett's Familiar Quotations*, 16th ed. (New York: Little Brown, 1992), 761.

38. Luke 22:42, KJV

39. Romans 8:38–39

ACKNOWLEDGMENTS

CHAPTER 1

"Being with God" by Jean Swensen. © 2002. Used by permission of the author.

"One Circle at a Time" by Evelyn D. Hamann. © 2002. Used by permission of the author.

CHAPTER 2

"Sixty-Two Dollars" by Nancy H. Cripe. © 2001. Used by permission of the author.

CHAPTER 3

"The Piano" by Sharon Sheppard. © 2001. Used by permission of the author.

"Those Cherry Macaroons" by Sharon M. Knudson. © 2002. Used by permission of the author. Sharon Knudson is a freelance writer and speaker in St. Paul, Minnesota, and has been published in a variety of periodicals.

"Dreams of Israel" (formerly titled "Rosy's Miracle") by Nancy Jo Sullivan. Adapted from *Moments of Grace* by Nancy Jo Sullivan. © 2000. Used by permission of Multnomah Publishers, Inc.

CHAPTER 4

"A Bouquet of Hope" by Nancy Jo Sullivan. © 2000. Used by permission of the author.

CHAPTER 5

"A Time to Die" by Carole Pearson. © 2002. Used by permission of the author.

"Happy Birthday, Baby Jesus" by Joanne M. Tarman. © 2002. Used by permission of the author.

CHAPTER 6

"Only a Dog" by Robert Dingman as told to Evelyn D. Hamann. © 2002. Used by permission.

"Such Small Matters for Prayer" by Joyce K. Ellis. © 2002. Used by permission of the author.

CHAPTER 7

"Thy Will Be Done" by John Gates. © 2002. Used by permission of the author.

"The Letter" by Dodie Davis. © 2002. Used by permission of the author.

CHAPTER 8

"Babies, Babies Everywhere" by Marlo Schalesky. From *Empty Womb, Aching Heart* by Marlo Schalesky. © 2001. Used by permission of Bethany House Publishers.

CHAPTER 9

"Under the Shadow of His Wings" by James F. Gauss. © 2001. Used by permission of the author. James F. Gauss is a freelance writer and speaker living in Minnesota. He is the author of *Christians Confronting Crisis* and the coauthor of *A Champion's Heart*. He may be reached at GHC@MNIC.net.

CHAPTER 10

"Thank God for the Fleas" by Corrie ten Boom with John and Elizabeth Sherrill. Adapted from *The Hiding Place.* © 1971, Chosen Books. Used by permission. All rights reserved.

"As the Waters Cover the Sea" by Noel Piper. © 2002. Used by permission of the author.

CHAPTER 11

"Don't Ever Forget" by Nancy Jo Sullivan. Adapted from *My Sister, My Friend,* by Nancy Jo Sullivan. © 2002. Used by permission of Multnomah Publishers, Inc.

STORIES OF ORDINARY PEOPLE AND AN EXTRAORDINARY GOD

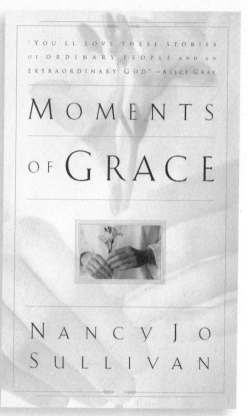

'YOU'LL LOVE THESE STORIES OF ORDINARY PEOPLE AND AN EXTRAORDINARY GOD' —ALICE GRAY

MOMENTS

OF GRACE

NANCY JO SULLIVAN

In this heartwarming volume, surprising true stories illustrate how normal people can move the mightiest mountain. A retired landscaper-turned-church-maintenance-man starts a nationally recognized ministry for the poor; a teenage girl offers comfort to a teacher who has just given birth to a Down syndrome baby; a tornado survivor grieves over two sisters lost in the storm, then dedicates her life to encouraging people who battle "the storms of life." These compelling stories offer encouraging proof that God will use any vessel—even the most ordinary.

ISBN 1-57673-698-9

SISTERS...

My Sister My Friend

Nancy Jo Sullivan *Photography by* Kathleen Francour

They share secrets and hairbrushes, crushes on the same boys, and clothes when the other isn't looking! Two lives linked by family—but so much more connects sisters to one another. Hearts entwine and dynamics unfold that create a bond unmatched by any other. It is a relationship of facets ranging from joy to heartache, the most lasting and endearing element being that of lifelong friends.

ISBN 1-57673-923-6